BWB Texts

Short books on big subjects from great New Zealand writers

The Interregnum
Rethinking New Zealand

Published in 2016 by Bridget Williams Books Limited, PO Box 12474, Wellington 6144, New Zealand, www.bwb.co.nz, info@bwb.co.nz. Reprinted 2016.

ISBN 9780947492649 (Paperback), ISBN 9780947492656 (EPUB), ISBN 9780947492663 (KINDLE), ISBN 9780947492670 (PDF)
ISTC A02201600000003A
DOI 10.7810/9780947492649

Acknowledgements
The publisher acknowledges the ongoing support provided by the Bridget Williams Books Publishing Trust.

Publisher: Tom Rennie
Editor: Max Rashbrooke
Cover and internal design: Base Two
Typesetter: Tina Delceg
Printer: Printlink, Wellington

CONTENTS

1. The Voices of a New Generation   8
    Morgan Godfery

2. Speech and Silence in the   23
    Public Sphere
    Andrew Dean

3. Reimagining the Economy   36
    Wilbur Townsend

4. Climate Change and Just Transition   51
    Edward Miller

5. Welfare and Precarious Work   65
    Chloe King

6. Radical Kaupapa Māori Politics   80
    Carrie Stoddart-Smith

7. Contributing to Public Life from Afar 97
    Lamia Imam

8. Feminism and Silence   112
    Holly Walker

9. Religion and the Real World   126
    Daniel Kleinsman

10. The Politics of Love   141
    Max Harris

Notes   154
About the Authors   166
About BWB Texts   170

VA SPACE VA'A SHIP

te waka
spirit vessel
breath carries
the ocean
birth
salt memory
forest
teu to keep
safe the va
shimmering
between us
teu
in flow
unending
from a single log
te waka
sacred star
niu night
calls
the rose
dawn

Courtney Sina Meredith

1. THE VOICES OF A NEW GENERATION

MORGAN GODFERY

'Stick close,' mutters a breathless activist, 'we're almost at Wellesley Street.' Roaming activists are moving from choke point to choke point in central Auckland, blocking roads to the city. 'This is a TPPA-free zone,' someone roars. Police come round the nearest corner. 'Here, sit down, sit down,' says a middle-aged man dressed in black, as the activists scramble to the middle of the intersection. Horns are blasting, probably in frustration rather than support, and more police begin arriving in squads. Officers in high-visibility vests circle the activists, though none seems willing to make a move. Journalists are the first to break the invisible line, pressing both sides on what they might do next. 'We are going to keep the blockade going,' answers one activist, while the police seem content to play cat and mouse as the city is paralysed. Few cars are making it through the blockades, and bus drivers are on strike for the day, so the only thing moving on Queen Street is a protest body more than 15,000-strong. 'Ka whawhai tonu mātou,' chants law professor Jane Kelsey from the back of a pick-up truck, electrifying the crowd. 'Ake, ake, ake,' they reply. Pedestrians are squeezing through the crowd; a young man in a suit asks what all the fuss is about. 'We are here to oppose the TPPA,' says a dark-haired Filipino woman. 'It attacks our sovereignty,' adds a young woman wearing her kura kaupapa Māori uniform. The TPPA they are opposing is the Trans-Pacific Partnership Agreement, the controversial twelve-nation trade agreement that triumphant government ministers are signing in a windowless conference room at SkyCity Grand Hotel, less than a block away from what protestors are describing as the largest direct action since the Springbok Tour in 1981.[1] The comfortable consensus on the merits of international trade agreements is beginning to fray, with the anti-TPPA Facebook likes coming to life as New Zealanders from all walks of life use their voice to either oppose or advocate for the deal. The morning papers are publishing comment pieces from opponents and advocates while 'TPPA' is the most popular search term on Google for the day. Comments on blog sites from across the political spectrum are numbering in the hundreds, while business leaders speaking on morning radio are suggesting that the opponents are working off misinformation, thanks to the government's poor 'sales job'. 'Free market capitalism is great,' says a counter-demonstrator on the corner of Customs Street and Queen Street, as Kelsey's pick-up truck creeps to a halt. The central city is jammed from end to end. From mid-morning to mid-afternoon on this day, 4 February 2016, the city belongs to the protestors. What started as a momentous day for trade ministers is ending as a referendum on their work.

To participate in politics is, for many young people, to experience powerlessness: no matter how many marches we organise, trade agreements are still signed. And if we find the courage to participate in public life, we are condemned as inveterate narcissists who prefer the comforts of 'virtue signalling' over the cold and remote logic of political pragmatism. 'Sensible' people ask why we persist with our pointless little rebellions, as if our political defeats demand private defeatism. Why bother marching against the TPPA while trade ministers are inking the deal? The answer, it seems to me, is twofold: history, the thing shaping our lives; and hope, the thing making it impossible to stay silent.

In regard to history, as Marx explains, we do not inherit the past 'under self-selected circumstances, but under circumstances existing already, given and transmitted from the past'. History is already organising the world as we find it, we merely inherit its triumphs and injustices. There is an element of tragedy here, captured in Fredric Jameson's remark that 'History is what hurts, it is what refuses desire and sets inexorable limits to individual as well as collective praxis.' But to guard against this fatalism – the idea that history is always set and our actions are irrelevant – we turn to the hope that history will not always repeat itself, or the hope that past injustices can be overcome. The Māori renaissance was an uprising against a grim history of economic inequality and cultural suppression, yet what made the movement possible and partly successful was the hope that the country was better than its past. Hope, coupled with the political struggle it demands, helped overturn more than a century of cultural suppression (we are still working on the inequality part). The same forces are at work in the movement against the TPPA: it involves a political struggle against the history the deal embeds, one that favours international corporate rights over domestic power; and hope – the thing that made the events of February 4th possible – for a political framework that favours individual and collective rights over corporate rights.

It is a compelling narrative, yet it avoids assigning agency: who is responsible for the history we are struggling against? There must be revolutionaries, so to speak, who are responsible for the status quo, from international trade agreements to austerity states. In the United States, Democratic presidential nominee Bernie Sanders blames the 'billionaire class' on Wall Street, while in the United Kingdom Labour party leader Jeremy Corbyn finds fault with City of London bankers, but New Zealanders need to look elsewhere – our revolutionaries were in government. Taking their inspiration from Margaret Thatcher's dramatic reforms in the United Kingdom, and exploiting the sense of crisis after prime minister Robert Muldoon mishandled the economy in the years up to 1984, the Fourth Labour Government leapt into a reform programme that we now call neoliberalism, the economic system and political rationality that replaced the old social democratic emphasis on price stability and full employment with an almost religious devotion to unregulated markets. But while their revolution delivered tremendous gains to the already rich, most New Zealanders found themselves worse off. This trend crystallised in the case of Telecom: thousands lost their jobs after it was privatised in 1990, but the consortium that acquired it walked away just seven years later with a profit of $7.2 billion.[2] More generally, salaried workers, having had their bargaining power cut since the 1990s, 'have lost around $19 billion a year, or $10,000 per wage earner per year, to the owners of capital,' writes Max Rashbrooke in *Wealth and New Zealand*. Meanwhile, the assets of our wealthiest 1 per cent increased from $94 billion to $147 billion between 2004 and 2010.[3] In New Zealand, as in other OECD countries, taxation has also become more regressive – that is, loading more of the tax burden on the poorest – especially since 2010, when the government generously reduced personal tax rates at the top while raising GST, which hits hardest in poor households.

This was not just a local phenomenon, though. Oxfam calculates that the world's wealthiest 1 per cent now own more assets than the rest of us combined;[4] in this light, the Occupy slogan 'we are the 99 percent' takes on a whole new meaning. With the benefit of hindsight, this was a predictable outcome of reducing top tax rates, opening borders for capital and not labour, and privatising public assets. The theorists, of course, predicted otherwise. The likes of Friedrich Hayek and Milton Friedman passionately argued that an economy with low taxes and private ownership would unleash our entrepreneurial imagination. We would all be producers and consumers and thought leaders. But most of us just remained ordinary old workers, except with diminished rights and poorer access to social security.[5] The rising tide did not lift all boats, only the 'super yachts,' as former Labour finance spokesperson David Parker put it.[6]

The argument for such political moves is usually that economic efficiency and investment will rise. But the opposite is true. Last year the United Nations Conference on Trade and Development found that the neoliberal revolution slowed growth rates and spurred unemployment, in effect reversing the remarkable growth in the industrialised world between the 1950s and 1970s.[7] That is neoliberalism's legacy: weaker growth and increased inequality.

Tragically, it is children who usually endure the greatest hardship. In 2015, 305,000 New Zealand children were living in poverty.[8] Yet, in our nostalgia for a supposed egalitarian past, we tend to forget that New Zealand has known intolerable levels of child poverty for a quarter of a century now. Following benefit cuts of 20 to 30 per cent in Ruth Richardson's 1991 'Mother of All Budgets', child poverty doubled almost overnight;[9] the children condemned to poverty in that year are adults now, perhaps with their own children in poverty.

Of course, most New Zealanders are enormously privileged, compared to many living in the developing world. But while we retain our global privileges, many of us are losing our local ones: new technology and new industrial centres are wiping out old jobs; the price of things like housing, commodities, currencies and stocks change rapidly; new and seemingly more dangerous non-state security threats are emerging; and the top-down media once thought to shape public opinion is disappearing. In other words, our economic and social worlds seem increasingly unstable as once reliable assumptions like a 'job for life' come under challenge. 'All fixed, fast-frozen relations, with their train of ancient and venerable prejudices and opinions, are swept away, all new-formed ones become antiquated before they can ossify,' wrote Marx and Friedrich Engels in 1848; '[a]ll that is solid melts into air.'[10]

The trouble for the neoliberal political settlement is that people are beginning to notice. We are living through a politics of protest and disruption, from Occupy to the movement against the TPPA. New populisms of the left and right are beginning to challenge the existing order: the Scottish National Party, Corbynism and UKIP nationalism in England; Spain's Podemos; the governing coalition of communist, social democratic and green parties in Portugal; perhaps even SYRIZA in Greece or Die Linke in Germany; certainly the Parti de Gauche and the Front National in France; arguably the Five Star Movement in Italy; definitely Black Lives Matter and the 'democratic socialism' of Bernie Sanders (and maybe the authoritarianism of Donald Trump) in the United States; maybe Idle No More (and to a lesser extent prime minister Justin Trudeau) in Canada; and undoubtedly Bolivarianism and indigenous movements in South America.

What is interesting here are the global links, the connectedness of these movements, which is fitting and necessary because neoliberalism is a system without a centre. One reason Occupy Wall Street spread across the world is that, in some senses, Wall Street is everywhere: capital knows no borders. It is easy to think that political upheaval is another country's problem and that we enjoy the benefit of stable government, but it could be argued that we, too, are entering a period of radical instability, and that politics is merely catching up. More and more New Zealanders seem to agree, including the 15,000 TPPA protestors who marched down Queen Street, the hundreds who blockaded central city intersections, and the thousands more who marched in other parts of the country, from Ruatoria to Whakatane, from Featherston to Wellington.

It seems that political struggle is back, acting as the bridge between a persistent sense of unfairness and the hope for something better, helping solve the antagonism between the historical and the utopian. 'The crisis consists precisely in the fact that the old is dying and the new cannot be born,' argued the Italian thinker Antonio Gramsci, '[and] in this interregnum a great variety of morbid symptoms appear.' The word interregnum implies that we are in a time of uncertainty, a space between dominant ideologies. This book argues that the interregnum can be confronted only through struggle, underpinned by love and but also a fierce desire to radically reshape politics. The centrepieces of late twentieth-century governance – a tax credit here, a royal commission there, a bold statement to the Press Gallery – are inadequate. Those left still using them might as well try to find their balance in a storm-whipped sea.

Nearly all of us are under pressure to approach life as a project in self-improvement, not necessarily for spiritual or intellectual development, but for survival in an increasingly competitive world. In between sending our snapchats and crafting our Facebook updates, life demands careful management. Is returning to university a worthwhile 'investment'? Is it possible to leverage one's hobby into a book deal? Is reading for knowledge or pleasure a waste of earning time? In *Undoing the Demos*, political theorist Wendy Brown describes how the market is reimaging life, disseminating 'market values' and metrics to every sphere of life and transforming humans from 'homo politicus' to 'homo economicus'.[11] Brown reinterprets

French theorist Michel Foucault's argument that neoliberalism transforms the individual into human capital, taking it a step further and reasoning that contemporary neoliberalism reconstitutes the individual as *financialised* human capital. Every aspect of life is seen as an opportunity for self-investment, competitive positioning, and realising value, with little room left for love. But the heart of Brown's critique is that neoliberalism undermines democracy. Where Foucault's key insight is that neoliberalism is more than an economic policy – it is a diffuse and deep restructuring of the state, its discourses and material practices – Brown goes one up and argues that neoliberalism restructures citizens too – and this in turn harms democracy.

Thinkers from Aristotle to John Locke have agreed, Brown argues, that there is a sacred space for the political in social life, a space not subject to the demands of economic rationality. This is where a democracy can prioritise deliberation, rights, duties and equality over the simple demands of economic gain or self-investment. But neoliberalism insists that individuals should maximise their human capital, and so homo politicus – that political person who values democracy – becomes homo economicus. The Latin terms lend a grandiose edge to the argument, yet it can be reduced to a simple question: rather than focusing on returns (monetary or not) on investment, perhaps we should approach politics for the sake of higher principles and values? This is precisely what the movement against the TPPA proclaims. The deal's advocates applaud the forecast gains, citing millions here, a per cent there, but its opponents are arguing on deeper premises. Opposition to the TPPA coheres around how it 'embeds' neoliberal history in our national policy. 'The accumulation of organising principles, instruments and institutions,' Kelsey argues, 'creates a regime so extensive, coherent and integrated that it cannot be transformed by simply reordering isolated elements.'[12] The TPPA, with its copyright extensions that protect monopoly power or its investor-state dispute settlement procedures that privilege corporate rights over domestic law-making, embeds central tenets of neoliberalism. This systematic opposition to neoliberalism, far from alienating New Zealanders or confusing them with its abstractions, works to unite different communities, from iwi to medical unions, and integrates their individual concerns into the whole. It signals a Foucauldian shift to understanding power as diffuse, and a revival of Brown's homo politicus in that the movement prioritises principles, values and analysis over purported gains.

But what is the role of writers here? Nearly every writer suspects his or her work is probably ephemeral, almost certainly insubstantial and guaranteed to register only with a privileged few. Against the urgency of tangible political struggle, writing can appear self-indulgent. But the interregnum, that ambiguous moment between society-wide discontent and political change, is not merely something to fight for – it is something to *think* through. It is up to writers to imagine a future shaped not by faceless historical forces alone, but by the agency of people acting together. And in bringing together a community to confront the world with bold demands for something new, writers can take us closer to this vision.

The writers you will meet here are determined to resist melancholy – the feeling that progress is better mourned than desired – and replace it with optimism, politics and love. Each writer, in their own way, sketches a future that unites communities, including the community you are meeting in this book; each of us, in a metaphorical way, is part of Courtney Sina Meredith's va'a, or waka, described in the poem that welcomes you to this work. We are in this together because the interregnum is not merely something that happens to us as a community or a country, instead it is something that we will help shape, but we have our own views on what that means and how it happens.

What we can agree on, as Andrew Dean argues, is that 'we have reached a point in our politics where questioning what the last three decades has wrought is an urgent necessity, but a point where such questions are only getting harder to ask.' Dean, who examines the world as our generation finds it, discovers a public sphere that neoliberalism has seriously undermined. That means confronting Gramsci's 'morbid symptoms' in a public forum is an enormous – and controversial – task. Yet Wilbur Townsend, Edward Miller and Chloe King meet the challenge, scrutinising precisely what the last three decades has wrought. Townsend surveys the current economy and investigates an alternative, Miller examines the politics and economics of climate change (perhaps the greatest threat to our future), and King takes on a work and welfare culture that has lost any sense of justice or love. It is this call for love that is the very heart of each contribution. Carrie Stoddard-Smith describes how aroha underpins kaupapa Māori politics (and its radical potential to reshape Aotearoa/New Zealand) while Holly Walker calls on Parliament to operate according to a new politics of love. Lamia Imam offers a vision of how to do so with current tools, while Daniel Kleinsman – drawing on Pope Francis and his recent encyclical on climate change – offers a new perspective to hold it all together, one that prioritises relationships of every kind over individual interests. At the close Max Harris takes love as his subject and imagines how it might reshape our politics and our lives. Rather than strive to maximise returns, what if we work to maximise happiness? Rather than calculate a worker's value, perhaps we should return to the idea that people are subjects who are ends in themselves, who have a value in themselves? Imagine a French peasant in 1787, one who is convinced that kings will rule in perpetuity, feudal lords will always starve the masses, and bishops will forever be at their intrigues. The peasant would have on his or her side the authority of history, the overpowering knowledge that nothing has changed in centuries, but he or she would be wrong about the direction history is travelling. It is up to us to ensure that history travels towards justice – and love.

2. SPEECH AND SILENCE IN THE PUBLIC SPHERE

ANDREW DEAN

At a literary festival in Jaipur in early 2015, Eleanor Catton, author of *The Luminaries*, told the audience that New Zealand was run by 'neoliberal, profit-obsessed, very shallow, very money-hungry politicians.' 'They care about short-term gains,' she said. 'They would destroy the planet in order to be able to have the life they want.'[1]

These comments caused what she would later describe as a 'jingoistic national tantrum,' one that ultimately involved broadcasters, politicians, journalists, and even her father.[2] Sean Plunket fomented national fury at her comments when he called her a 'traitor' and an 'ungrateful hua' on his radio programme. 'Oh that's nice Eleanor,' he said, 'given that you've got a job that's all about culture, that's paid for by the taxpayer! So Eleanor Catton, stick that where the sun don't shine!'[3] Nor was Prime Minister John Key impressed with Catton's remarks; he commented to media that it was 'a bit sad really that she's mixing politics with some other things that she's better-known for'.[4] 'I don't think that reflects what most New Zealanders perceive of the Government,' Key told reporters, professedly saddened that 'she doesn't have respect for the work that we do, because I have tremendous respect for what she does as a writer.'[5]

Catton's father, Philip, responded in an interview to Key and Plunket's comments. On Plunket's Radio Live show, Philip Catton told the radio host: 'You are a father ... you have disappointed me in the approach that you have taken.' Plunket, Catton said, had impoverished public debate with his name-calling, failing to 'advance towards a reckoning, a respectful reckoning of differences of ideas'.[6]

Writing in the *Pantograph Punch* some months later, Philip Catton reflected on the deeper meaning of the way his daughter's comments had been received. Centring on the notion of 'respect'– the Prime Minister's apparent 'respect' for Eleanor Catton's work – Philip argued that for Key this value operated according to a market-oriented rather than a truth-oriented form of reasoning. Such an orientation was no accident, he continued, suggesting that it reflected both the economic changes of the last thirty years and the ideas that support them. In this spirit, he wrote that our current political situation promotes 'self-dependency' over 'interdependency,' and that life is transformed into a 'competitive game' where we seek to 'get ahead of the others, economically'. In public debate this leads us to compete rather than to learn, to argue on the basis of what we may gain for ourselves rather than the truth we may discover. His daughter's 'criticism could be relevant only if in some contest of power with [Key] she were liable to win'.[7]

There are few things less edifying than the sight of the Prime Minister telling a citizen to get out of politics, or listening to a hurt father publicly defend his daughter from accusations that she is 'ungrateful' and a 'traitor'. Of course, the outrage to which Eleanor Catton was subjected was manufactured for reasons that had little to do with her, what she had to say about New Zealand, or the government funding she received; instead it had everything to do with the use to which she could be put. Plunket generated a national debate about 'our' writers and their responsibilities, and installed himself at the centre of it; Key claimed that Eleanor Catton's statement 'probably summarises the Green Party view of this Government,' not missing the chance to link his politics with what it means to be a New Zealander.[8] These kinds of motivations are the competitive element to which Philip Catton referred in his article: neither Key nor Plunket had any stake in advancing the reckoning of ideas even if it is quite clear that they should have, and their contributions were never designed to add anything positive to the conversation.

For all of the bluster, the saga was, in fact, instructive. For a brief moment, criticism of the direction of the nation's politics was united with criticism of the nation's public sphere. We saw how our politics and the way that we talk about them in public are both organised by the very forces of which Eleanor and Philip Catton were critical; that is, the history and practice of neoliberalism. These politics and this debate occupy the remainder of this chapter.

New Zealand, like many other countries across the globe, has undergone a total overhaul of its politics and economy over the last three decades. The theories that drove the changes, derived for the most part from a small band of American economists, propose that free markets are always the most efficient mechanisms for distributing goods (including social goods such as health care and welfare) and that human development is best progressed in an environment where individuals are freely able to enter into market relations with others. In their ascendency these ideas have become increasingly ambitious. Free market economics is now imagined to be some kind of 'science of human behaviour', in the words of the philosopher Michael Sandel: 'In all domains of life, human behaviour can be explained by assuming that people decide what to do by weighing the costs and benefits of the options before them, and choosing the one they believe will give them the greatest welfare, or utility.'[9] The implications of these ideas for the state have been manifest in the years since 1984: the state has endeavoured to organise as many areas of life as possible in terms of 'efficient' market systems, and has redesigned its institutional structures accordingly.

This model of economic organisation swept across the world in the 1970s and 1980s. Following General Augusto Pinochet's military coup in 1973, Chile became the first state to incorporate neoliberal ideas across its economy. Free marketeer Milton Friedman and his Chilean disciples, known as the 'Chicago Boys', directed the restructuring, as the new government privatised public assets and social security, opened up resource extraction to private enterprise, encouraged foreign investment and crushed trade unions.[10] The election of Margaret Thatcher in 1979 and Ronald Reagan in 1980 saw the beginnings of similar processes in the United Kingdom and the United States, as both leaders moved their nations away from social democratic post-war compromises, choosing, in

Pinochet's words, 'proprietors' over 'proletarians.'

New Zealand's development is a part of this global history. In the decade from 1984, successive governments restructured the economy along the same lines as Thatcher, Reagan and Pinochet. Within the space of a few years, New Zealand was transformed from one of the most protected economies in the western world to one of the least. Two ministers of finance – one from Labour, one from National – programmatically pulled government back from involvement in the economy and in people's lives, selling state assets, slashing personal income taxes and giving over important elements of economic management to the Reserve Bank.[11] At the same time, they attacked unions, cut welfare, removed agricultural and manufacturing subsidies, and created markets in higher education, health care, public housing and other public goods. By the time Ruth Richardson was dumped as Minister of Finance in 1993, New Zealand had become, in Jane Kelsey's words, 'the darling of the world's free-marketeers', and international observers were speaking of the 'New Zealand model' of economic reform.[12] In the years that followed, the architects of these changes toured the world promoting their successes, and international business periodicals praised the country's 'courage' and 'leadership'. New Zealand had been changed forever.

It is to both this history and these ideas that Philip Catton was referring in his various comments, as he attempted to count the costs of what has taken place. There was sadness in his voice when he reflected on the world that he saw every day on 'the streets of Wellington,' beyond the Radio Live studio: 'I walk to work. I see two homeless people on my way to work. People packing their belongings into that kind of cloth bag that is attached to wheels.' His work colleagues were faring little better: they 'starve themselves up to Christmas time because they want to provide some festivities [for] their children,' he reflected, and they 'lose their teeth because they can't afford the cost of a root canal'. These 'impressions', he said, had led him to become 'highly aware … of things the market doesn't do, hasn't done, and, at the same time, enormously depends upon'. Such impressions also made him question 'the neoliberal ideas about the market as an important force behind all good in the world'.[13]

Yet Catton's ruminations fell on deaf ears. Even as his interviewee was making these observations, Plunket sought to engage him in a contest, to determine where it was that he stood, to fight to win. 'I'm here to talk with you about ideas, and about the discussion of ideas and how you've derailed it', Catton said, frustrated with the way the conversation was going. Plunket spoke over him to ask, 'So you're against neoliberalism?'[14]

Looking back in his *Pantograph Punch* article some months later, Catton offered some suggestions as to why the argument – if it may be called that – proceeded in the terms that it did. 'Recent political history', he wrote, had turned against the project of thinking together in the pursuit of truth. Our nation's trajectory toward 'ever-increasing inequality' was producing the very opposite of the 'equalisation of power' that was a precondition for the 'ideal of inclusive reasoning'.[15] His remarks imply that in an environment of enormous disparity, we are left with a public sphere that operates unequally, silencing some while privileging others.

Not listening, or refusing to listen, marks our treatment of those who have been disempowered by the changes of the last three decades. The standard we are left with in public discourse is exclusive, a form of dominance. Even in elections, where we are told every vote is equal, the pattern remains. Data from the New Zealand General Social Survey show that those who said they did not have enough money were more than twice as likely not to vote in the 2011 election than those who said they had more than enough to meet their everyday needs.[16] The unemployed were similarly less likely to vote, despite the enormous impact government has on their lives.[17] Even Sean Plunket seemed to recognise the decreasing participation that marks

New Zealand's contemporary politics when he told Philip Catton, at the end of the interview, that if he had his 'time again' he would not say 'that Eleanor should stay out of politics'. He added: 'In a democracy everyone should be involved in politics, and part of the problem with our democracy is a lot of people aren't, for various reasons.'[18]

These 'various reasons' are a matter of structure and design. Foundational to the changes of the 1980s and 1990s were principles that sought to limit citizens' role in economic decision-making. The Reserve Bank Act 1989 first enshrined in legislation the bank's independence from political supervision, and then defined 'price stability' as the Bank's primary objective – two decisions which in effect ensured that the ideology of the reformers was not up for democratic deliberation. The Employment Contracts Act 1991 put an end to the era of large-scale union negotiation, sending the membership of these workers' organisations into freefall in the following years, and dramatically eroding the ability of workers to have a stake either in the negotiation of their own conditions and wages or in the structure of the economy more generally.

The way that the assumptions of the reforms have redefined the boundaries of our politics is nowhere clearer than in universities, which, alongside unions, have been a traditional home for political debate and dissent. The final embedding of the reforms was the 'discipline' Ruth Richardson sought to bring to bear on these state institutions: by tying funding directly to a formula based on enrolments, she ensured that universities were responsive to 'signals' from 'consumers' – that is, students. Universities and eventually departments were made to compete for numbers in order to remain viable. This transition redefined the value that a university provides in narrow terms of student interest and satisfaction, a point that was not lost on faculty at the time but which they had little choice about if they wished to keep their jobs. Their traditional 'critic and conscience' role was enormously diminished in these years, circumscribed by what was economically rational.

It was not just faculty who were affected by the new system: students over the last two-and-a-half decades have found that university funding militates against their participation in political debate. The 1991 Budget saw significant cuts to student benefits as well as the introduction of a strict parental means test for all those under the age of 25. To cover the costs that students now faced, which included uncapped tuition fees, a student loan scheme was introduced; by 2014 it had had over 1.2 million people on its books.[19] Paying for university forces students to focus on the value their education will have in the labour market and how they will be able to pay off their loan, rather than the kind of thinking to which they might be exposed, or the way their education might bring about self-development. Market discipline here is also a form of political and mental discipline: most students do not have the time to think about the way things could be when they are worrying about the way things are. It seems entirely unsurprising now that one of the last bastions of union strength in New Zealand, the student unions, recently had their power diminished by the introduction of compulsory voluntary membership – just one more to add to the many restrictions on young people thinking, speaking, and acting together in the public sphere.

Another major institution, public broadcasting, has seen its mission directed toward similar ends. The deregulation of broadcasting under theFourth Labour Government brought private companies into competition with public ones. Television New Zealand was recast as a commercial operation expected to return dividends to the Crown, and, like universities, the primary metric of public broadcasters' success has become an economic one, in this case the value TVNZ is able to derive from selling its audiences to advertisers. This competitive commercial environment encourages hosts like Plunket to attempt to generate the kind of controversy that they do, with the aim of increasing ratings, irrespective of what these interventions wreak.

It is not, of course, that people have stopped talking and caring about politics. It is that the reforms drastically reduced the power of certain institutions to organise dissent. The process has been one of active silencing. In New Zealand, this included unions, universities, and broadcasting among others. In Britain, Thatcher's targets were organisations that augured a different way of structuring the world, unions and particular local councils she perceived as being too left-wing. This is part of the story of how the ideologies of the reformers became embedded, and how their assumptions about the economy and even the way people are became an invisible form of common-sense. It is a story too about the kind of public sphere we have where Eleanor Catton's ideas could be unimaginable, and about the way that she was swiftly silenced. The call by Plunket and Key for Eleanor Catton to stay out of politics creates little dissent in a public sphere uninterested in democracy or, as Philip Catton lamented, something as radical as 'truth'. Silencing those who would be critical is a strategy of long standing, as we have seen, and the attacks on the author of *The Luminaries* were merely its latest ugly manifestation.

The problem for those who would attack her, though, is that public debate is never finished, and the public sphere is still created in the process of speaking, writing and thinking – we are all doing it, all the time, and we can all break open this world, little by little. It was in a spirit of defiance that Eleanor Catton suggested in an interview with the *Guardian* that 'eloquence, imagination, and reasoned debate' may counter the attacks on her, and that these are 'qualities ... that persist, and will continue to persist, despite efforts to humiliate and silence those who speak out'.[20] There is still room for something better to arise out of this shabby affair, and it has been part of the project of this chapter to move the conversation along. There is no doubt that we have reached a point in our politics where questioning what the last three decades have wrought is an urgent necessity, but it is a point where such questions are only getting harder to ask. We must ask nonetheless, with the radicalism of eloquence and imagination.

3. REIMAGINING THE ECONOMY

WILBUR TOWNSEND

The week I finished high school I moved to Lower Hutt and was made a labourer in a scaffolding firm. It was a good job – regular hours, paid a couple of dollars more than the minimum wage, taught me the difference between the Layher system and tube-and-clip, and showed me parts of the city you don't normally get to see: million-dollar apartments on Oriental Parade, mid-renovation council flats in Newtown, the inside of the Whittaker's chocolate factory.

Most important were the blokes I worked with. There was a big Samoan guy who squeezed himself into the yard's forklift every morning. I'd perch on his forks and he'd chuckle, lifting me to return some steel to an out-of-reach shelf, the two of us looking like the warning cartoons you see in health and safety manuals. There was a skinny Pākehā who was always worrying about the drug tests – he was easy to get along with, provided you didn't question his scaffolding or the length of the bakery breaks he'd take on the way to site. And there was Pat, an old Māori man who'd been with the firm as long as anyone.[1] Pat's back wasn't holding up too well but his son – who the others reckoned could scaffold before he could write – had set him up with pen-pushing work to pay the bills until he hit sixty-five. He still ended up on site more often than he should've. I remember him chatting to me when the two of us were out working on those council flats. 'Reckon I'll get one of those house buses when I retire, eh. Spend my years with the missus on the road.'

When I left the firm to start university they let me keep the overalls and steel-caps, telling me to come back the next summer. But when I did, they were laying off permanent staff and couldn't take anyone on. I didn't take it personally; I was hardly the only bloke off the building site that summer. Some 175,000 New Zealanders were employed in construction during the first three months of 2010,[2] but only 160,000 were a year later.

The number of construction jobs has since increased – earthquakes and housing bubbles have that much to say for them – but the secure, traditionally masculine, low or medium-skill work that construction typifies has long been in decline. When Jim Bolger was elected prime minister in November 1990, 10.4 per cent of the country's jobs were in agriculture, forestry or fishing.[3] Now 5.9 per cent are.[4] In 1990, 18.8 per cent of the country's jobs were in manufacturing; now only 10.6 per cent are.[5] They have been replaced by service jobs – in health care, recreation and tourism, hospitality – which tend to be paid less and are casualised, with weaker unions.

The result is that a decreasing share of New Zealand's growth is finding its way into pay cheques. Per person, after accounting for inflation, the New Zealand economy earnt 48 per cent more in 2015 than it did in 1990.[6] Over that time the average wage has grown by 22 per cent.[7] Much of that wage growth has been in finance and insurance, where pay is 62 per cent higher. Wages in retail have grown by 12 per cent; wages in hospitality by only 3 per cent. When we consider the economy as an anonymous aggregate we find that it's healthy, it's growing, there's more money being earned in this country each year than there was in the last. But when we consider workers' individual material existences, we find ourselves contradicted. There is money being earned in this country but, increasingly, it isn't being earned by us.

THE ROBOTS ARE STEALING OUR JOBS

There's an Italian restaurant in India where they deliver your pizza by drone. They put a video of it online – you can watch the pimply delivery boy become obsolete while rock music and Martin Luther King Jr samples play in the background. Domino's is building the DomiCopter, while a takeaway restaurant in Beijing reckons drones have cut their delivery times in half. I remember when the self-service machine was introduced in the local New World back in 2008; my mates who worked on checkout were assured no jobs were in danger. But between the 2006 and 2013 censuses the number of checkout operators in New Zealand decreased by 6.4 per cent.[8] Last October McDonald's introduced self-service machines into their Lower Hutt restaurants. An MP I follow on Twitter described them as 'phenomenal'.

We normally blame either partisan politics or some grand impression of neoliberal ideology for the changes in the labour market, but in truth the changes in New Zealand have echoed changes in other rich countries. Even in the great Nordic social democracies the old jobs are disappearing. Over 21 per cent of Denmark's jobs were in manufacturing in 1992, but only 12.5 per cent in 2014.[9] The International Labour Organisation has data for Norway and Sweden only from 1996, when 15.8 per cent of Norwegian jobs and 20.1

per cent of Swedish jobs were in manufacturing. By 2014 those figures had dropped to 9.7 per cent and 11.2 per cent. The cause isn't ideological. The cause is a shifting mechanics in the means of production.

Economic research on the effects of new technology has largely focused on whether the technologies are *labour-augmenting* or *capital-augmenting* – whether they increase the productivity of labour or capital. But talk of labour-augmenting and capital-augmenting technologies is becoming irrelevant. Robotification doesn't magnify labour and capital, it blurs them, it lets them perform the same role. In the economist's lexicon, technology is now increasing the *elasticity of substitution* between labour and capital.

This distinction is important. Think of the caricature painted of those who question the liberating potential of technology: they're called Luddites, a reference to English weavers who between 1811 and 1816 set fire to the steam-powered looms that were replacing them. Historical inaccuracies aside (the Luddites were more interested in industrial negotiations than in halting technological change), the Luddites make for a powerful symbol. The industrial revolution was a necessary precursor to the society we live in today, a society which – for all its ills – provides a standard of living that even British royalty couldn't have imagined two hundred years ago. In threatening the development of that society, the Luddites seem myopic to the point of blindness.

But there's a difference between steam-powered looms and self-service checkouts. Steam-powered looms increased the quantity of cloth a worker could produce, a classic case of labour-augmenting technology. At first, firms used the new technology to produce the same amount of cloth with fewer workers, sacking the workers the steam-powered looms had made redundant. But the steam-powered looms also increased the productivity of the remaining workers. As the sacked workers found new jobs, workers' increasing productivity increased their industrial power, and that – eventually – empowered them to demand higher wages. Technology that made workers more productive eventually made workers more powerful. It's naïve to hope that robotification, which makes workers completely unnecessary, will do the same.

As technology blurs the distinctions between labour and capital, the sheer quantity of capital has multiplied: we have more tractors and factories and brutalist apartment blocks than ever. In 1950 British capital was worth about £40 billion.[10] By 2010 it was worth over £8 trillion – almost eight times as much, after controlling for inflation. American capital was seven times more valuable in 2010 than it was in 1950, French capital nine times. Wherever we have the data to measure it – unfortunately not in New Zealand – we find that capital grew faster than the economies that produced it.

The effect of this massive expansion in the scale of capital will depend on how labour and capital interact in global production. If labour and capital occupy distinct roles – if their elasticity of substitution is low – more capital means more competition between capitalists for an increasingly overcrowded niche. Even as they own more machines the capitalists will find those machines earning them a decreasing share of global income. However, if labour and capital occupy similar roles, labour must also compete with the new capital, and so increasing quantities of capital will also increase the capitalists' share of income.

As machines become robots, capital will be released from its narrow economic niche. The accumulation of capital will no longer threaten the capitalists. Capital will become a beast, each year growing stronger as each year it grows larger.

MAYBE THE ROBOTS AREN'T STEALING ALL OF OUR JOBS

As the distinctions between worker and machine have rusted we have taken to the worker with a new chisel, hoping to expose limbs the machine does not yet possess. If there will be no more delivery boys then we must transform the delivery boys into mechanical engineers or aged-care workers or writers of pop culture think pieces. We will restore the worker's humanity by giving them capacities a machine cannot emulate.

Unfortunately, any strategy to transform delivery boys into mechanical engineers requires that those delivery boys pass a mechanical engineering course. The twenty-first-century careers we hear so much about – computer science, data science, engineering – require long periods of difficult study. Our utopian imagination finds it easy to grab the truckies made redundant by self-driving trucks and plonk them behind AutoCAD terminals or C++ compilers. Learning the statically-typed programming and Boolean logic and graph-searching algorithms will be a little more difficult.

The robots are unlikely to take every unskilled job in the country. New Zealand's aging population and scientists' surprising inability to digitise empathy has, over the past 25 years, doubled the number of jobs classified by Statistics New Zealand as 'Health Care and Social Assistance' – the caring industries.[11] Unfortunately, putting the truckies on toilet-cleaning duty in the local rest home is as sensible as putting the truckies through an engineering degree. Workers in the caring industries are disproportionately women.

Misogynistic workplaces, sexist bosses and male-designed career paths discourage women from many low or medium-skill jobs; that's why we still see few female truckies, wharfies, chippies or sparkies. This increases competition for jobs traditionally staffed by women. That competition has flattened wages in the caring industries down to their legal minimums, and has provided employers in these industries with a long list of women they can call on when they need more staff. Employers who can siphon from the large pool of underemployed female labour are unlikely to have much use for truckies with dirty mouths and grubby tattoos and living wage expectations.

The truth is that not all labouring bodies constructed for the current world of work can be adjusted to the demands of the next. If we are to avoid an economy of redundancy and WINZ service centre queuing, our focus must switch from adjusting bodies to adjusting the system which allocates those bodies their value. To shirk from that task is to acquiesce to economic tragedy. But before we ready our placards and Change.Org petitions, a careful examination of that tragedy is necessary. The tragedy would not be the destruction of those good old stable jobs. The tragedy would be forgetting that the destruction is something to celebrate.

IF ONLY THE ROBOTS WOULD STEAL OUR JOBS

We worship the Good Job: the guaranteed hours, the fifteen minutes for smoko and the half hour for lunch. Even as our best hours are taken from us, we rejoice at compensation that is little more than a smidgen of our worth, a Stockholm syndrome of thankful labour. The worship can be justified as long as good jobs are all we can imagine. But as soon as the job is proven unnecessary, that worship becomes idolatry. When we yearn for stable work we are yearning for a stable pay cheque, and if we could take the pay cheque without the work we would. The roboticised economy is only as dystopian as our social institutions allow it to be. Yes, it has the potential to be an economy of redundant labour. But it also has the potential to make labouring redundant, to let us no longer be defined by the output we produce.

Designing socio-economic institutions that let people *not* work is fairly easy. Every week, you give everybody money. You give them that money regardless of whether or not they work. People think to themselves, 'Neat: now that I have money, I am less sad about not being able to work.' A universal income makes labouring voluntary – we can still earn our wages by labouring if we want to, but by having a portion of our income independent of our labouring, we can retain our humanity when the economy is no longer dependent on us.

Some people will leave the rat race and move to Takaka. They'll even refer to it as 'the rat race', no irony in their voice as they blather on, half-baked, pausing only to puff on a comically proportioned bong. This is okay. As uncomfortable as it might make us, people have the right to find their own meaning for their lives, even if they insist on looking for that meaning within snap-lock fitty-bags. A universal income will let us live a life that matches our values, a life no longer restricted by the values of the market.

Others will stay working. The universal income will shelter the aged-care workers and engineers from the flood of newly redundant labour. If they are sacked, the universal income will let them spend longer searching for their next job, waiting for an offer that matches their worth. By calming the desperation of unemployment the universal income will provide workers an option for a life outside the workforce. That option will strengthen them, even if they have no intention of using it.

A universal income that allows a life outside the workforce would have to be large enough to live off. And the problem with giving everybody large amounts of free money is that doing so could become expensive. If you add up the spending a universal income would replace – superannuation, student allowances, Working for Families, the dole, and so on – you get to roughly $20 billion a year.[12] That amounts to $90 a week per New Zealander – certainly not enough to live off. While we could all point to some government programmes we consider unnecessary (I would dismantle the military), we tend to disagree about what those programmes are, and in any case they will never amount to the many billions of dollars a universal income requires.

Thankfully there's plenty more money for us to grab, if we're willing to reach for it. One of the ways our government statisticians calculate GDP is by tallying the annual incomes of every person in the country. In doing so, they determine whether the income was received by labour (salaries and wages) or by capital (rents, profits and interest). Capital received $72 billion in 2015, less than a third of which is already taxed.[13] There's plenty to be grabbed at. The only difficulty is in determining the appropriate claw.

If this is to be the century of ascendant capital, an obvious option is to socialise private capital and return the means of production – the factories, the machines, the raw materials – to the collective. The historians insist that this tends to work poorly but I suspect they just haven't noticed it done well. State ownership of the means of production didn't end in 1991 – Norway's sovereign wealth fund is worth $1.3 trillion and Abu Dhabi's $1.2 trillion.[14] Of course the Norges Bank doesn't exactly operate by Five Year Plan, but then one of the great successes of twentieth-century capitalism was separating management from ownership and there's no reason why socialism shouldn't do the same.

Critics of socialised production are always happy to explain why centrally planned economies stagnate, but they only ever provide a critique of state-*managed* production, never a critique of state-*owned* production. Global capitalism has already discarded the patrilineal corporate legacies. Big companies are rarely managed by their owners; they're managed by professional executives. Those executives can be left in management when sovereign wealth funds own the companies. Admittedly, executive management will prevent socialised production from solving all of capitalism's problems. Thankfully, socialised production will still solve the biggest: that the rewards of our machine age are being taken by the few who own the machines. If we own the machines through our sovereign wealth funds, the income they earn can be made a universal income.

Socialism can be more than marching Cossacks and centrally dictated production quotas. By socialising capital within sovereign wealth funds, socialism can emulate capitalist dynamism without emulating its callous sense of value.

WE MUST ENSURE THE ROBOTS STEAL OUR JOBS

It's easy to romanticise the satisfaction of hard yakka, to tint the sepia a little brighter as we twiddle with the filters of our national consciousness. It's difficult to remember that good hard work is still work, that it's a rare sod who clocks in at the start of their day without something else they'd rather be doing. That job I had scaffolding, it was a good job. But when I think back to that scaffolding yard I can't think of a single bloke who'd have stayed there if he won Powerball. You saw it in the lingering bakery breaks. We took a few minutes more than necessary to finish our ciggy or chicken and chips. We laid out blueprints for the hours we hadn't sold, planned our evening or our weekend or our summer holiday. *Reckon I'll get one of those house buses when I retire, eh. Spend my years with the missus on the road.*

As we reimagine this economy, we mustn't imagine workers in the same tired old hierarchy, only now surrounded by more blinking LED lights. We can be more than our nostalgia, we can dream beyond the stable, well-paid and completely soulless jobs of the twentieth century. Economic relations still determine social relations: 'The hand-mill gives you society with the feudal lord; the steam-mill, society with the industrial capitalist.'[15] Perhaps the quadrocopter drone can give us a society which defines us by more than our job. That would certainly be a society worth working for.

4. CLIMATE CHANGE AND JUST TRANSITION

EDWARD MILLER

'If there is any hope for the world, it does not live in climate-change conference rooms or in cities with tall buildings.' – Arundhati Roy[1]

In an unexpected twist of fate, I recently found myself spending a few days in the non-governmental organisation (NGO) space of the 2015 Paris climate talks, an enormous conference centre adjacent to where the talks were taking place. The gravity of the event was unmistakeable. Following the tragic Paris terror attacks some weeks before, transport routes to official venues were lined with heavily armed riot police; hovering drone cameras surveilled key locations; and some radical activists were kept under house arrest for the duration of the talks, ostensibly because of the national state of emergency. Global weather events played up for the occasion as well. The El Niño pattern of 2015 meant the talks had for their backdrop South Africa's worst drought since 1982, some of Britain's worst-ever floods, forest fires in Australia, recording-breaking Christmas temperatures in the United States, and yet another super-typhoon in the central Philippines.

The deal struck at Paris was one that enabled heads of state to applaud each other's generous diplomacy, knowing full well that while the aspirational target of holding global temperature increases to 1.5C sounded great, national commitments could still take temperatures to an increase of between 2.7C and 3.5C.[2] No matter how weak or strong the concluded text might be, the deeply held commitment of large businesses and governments to maintaining economic growth at all costs appeared to have shaped the agenda. Reaching the 1.5C target is now becoming increasingly difficult as a cocktail of financial and geopolitical factors have sent hydrocarbon prices into a downward spiral, giving large corporates increasing access to cheap fossil fuels. Carbon credit markets, which are supposed to set a price that drives de-carbonisation, remain in the doldrums. How we can prevent these market signals from decimating the agreement's target remains unclear.

I write this not as seasoned climate change campaigner, but as a trade unionist and political activist with a keen interest in global justice. Climate change is not another political issue to be managed. The transition to a low-carbon economy requires a new vision of economic development, a transition that puts the interest of the most vulnerable first. As we enter the interregnum, the cracks in neoliberalism's ideological armour are beginning to show. This chapter is an attempt to highlight some of those cracks and, in some small way, articulate a way to resist the dominant political narrative. These are our battles, and unless we muster the requisite political will to fight them we stand to lose everything.

NEOLIBERAL WONDERLAND BURNING

'In the Business Roundtable view, a serious attempt to block greenhouse gas emissions globally would give new legs to a regulatory agenda that they were trying to kill off.' – Bryan Gould[3]

New Zealand's climate change policy still carries the imprint of the neoliberal experiments of the 1980s and '90s. Neoliberalism's articles of faith comprise liberal trade and investment policies, financial and labour market deregulation, privatisation of state assets and cuts to public spending. These policies, as carried out in New Zealand, have engendered a massive upward transfer of wealth, empowering finance capital to shape the political discourse. On a psychological level, neoliberalism has embedded baseline assumptions around the values that policy-making should protect: individualism, private property rights and the primacy of the free market.[4] This has resulted in a weak set of climate change policies that allow polluters, particularly in the agricultural sector, to eschew their responsibilities and transfer costs to the most vulnerable in society.

New Zealand's recent history of climate change policy begins in 1997 when it signed the Kyoto Protocol, committing itself to reduce emissions to 1990 levels between 2008 and 2012. The nation was going to do something; the question was what. Political debate demonstrated the limited scope of acceptable discussion: the more ambitious camp favoured a direct tax on carbon, while free marketeers argued for the establishment of a market in carbon credits. The latter camp had ample financial resources, manufacturing bespoke lobby groups like the Greenhouse Policy Commission (comprising many of the country's largest polluters) and working to kill off the carbon tax policy option. Business lobby groups like the Business Roundtable sponsored a steady stream of speakers championing business-friendly policy mechanisms (as well as a plethora of climate deniers, like the NZ Climate Science Coalition) to delay and shape the debate.[5]

By 2013 New Zealand was producing almost 25 per cent more greenhouse gases than in 1990,[6] while lobby groups had limited discussion to the more market-friendly carbon-trading approach. Global warming had all but disappeared, according to distorted data presented by the lobby groups, and the more interventionist carbon tax approach was no longer necessary. In 2008 the outgoing Labour Government established the Emissions Trading Scheme (ETS). It was riddled with holes from the outset: the ETS was supposed to be a 'cap and trade' system, where emitters (like factories or farmers) were required to surrender carbon credits equivalent to their emissions, while carbon sinks (like forest owners) were allocated emission credits. However, the scheme had no 'cap' or limit to the number of credits in the domestic market, rendering prices vulnerable to collapse or fluctuation. It was also stacked with 'transitional' measures, including free credit allocations, a two-for-one system that halved most emitters' initial financial liability, and the exclusion of pastoral agriculture which was responsible for almost half of New Zealand's emissions until 2013.

In the year 2008 Lehman Brothers collapsed and the United States subprime mortgage crisis went global, oil prices hit an all-time high of

US$151 a barrel and New Zealand inked its free trade agreement with China. Here, the financial crisis affected second-tier lenders, notably South Canterbury Finance, which received a $1.8 billion bailout; but New Zealand's Australian-owned banks received a government guarantee and had limited exposure to the kind of toxic debt that affected the transatlantic financial houses. Skyrocketing Chinese demand for New Zealand agricultural commodities, rising oil prices, and populist fears of market instability gave a powerful pretext for the National Government to reduce the burden of the ETS on business.

In November 2009, the government amended the ETS to delay the entry of agriculture to the scheme until January 2015. It also changed the free allocation of carbon credits (New Zealand Units) to an 'intensity' basis. Firms received more credits if they increased their output, so long as the intensity of emissions dropped. This effectively acted as a subsidy for big polluters. Persistently high fossil fuel prices gave ample pretext for the government to open up new mining and drilling frontiers which, despite some of the largest protests seen in decades, were regarded by many middle-class voters as being inextricably linked to New Zealand's future economic success.[7] Few who had followed the debate closely were surprised when gross emissions overshot our initial Kyoto target by 20 per cent, requiring the government to use its credits from pre-existing forests to meet the commitment.

Under the second Kyoto phase, New Zealand had committed to a non-binding pledge to reduce emissions 5 per cent below 1990 levels between 2013 and 2020, a target the Ministry for the Environment predicts we will overshoot by 46 per cent.[8] It is important to note that there is no current policy proposal to meet these targets, save a few token investments in dealing with agricultural emissions. It was this faltering ambition, coupled with fears of a 'double-dip' global financial crisis, that prompted New Zealand's announcement in late 2012 that it was pulling out of the Kyoto process altogether (as were other developed Anglo-American nations). While not unexpected, this symbolic gesture was indicative of New Zealand's position on tackling climate change: it was not willing to sacrifice economic growth to achieve a set of policy aims that other countries, particularly large developing ones like China and India, were doing little to address.

In 2012 the National Government introduced legislation to further minimise the impact of the ETS on business, stretching out 'transitional' measures from the 2008 legislation against the advice of the 2012 independent review. The total effect of these changes was that the ETS now failed to create the incentives and disincentives for industries to stay within the national carbon budget.[9] The fledgling ETS had been broken. By April 2013, when the law passed, campaigners had little ammunition left to change popular opinion. Although more and more young people were becoming absorbed by the issue, the dominance of the market paradigm made alternative solutions difficult to articulate. By mid-2014 fossil fuel prices began a downward slide. Some blamed the Saudis and other Middle Eastern oil nations for refusing to cut production quotas, and while this surely did not help the situation, the reality is that major oil firms overinvested in supply while persistent economic crises meant world demand fell. Oil became cheap, if only we could afford it.

In 2015, the government began consulting the public on the emissions reductions targets it would put forward at the Paris talks. Its consultation document was primarily designed to justify a low target, proposing a number of grounds for why New Zealand could not set a more ambitious one: we already have significant renewable electricity generation; the largest part of our emissions comes from agriculture (and, it is argued, nothing can be done quickly in that area); and we have a relatively sparse population density. The government clearly hung its hopes on a certain kind of fix: technology was mentioned thirty-two times on the presumption that an entrepreneurial economy that encouraged innovation could magic away the fundamentals of climate science. Of the 17,000 submitters, 99 per cent demanded an emissions target of 40 per cent or more below 1990 levels.[10] The target the government submitted to the Paris talks was an 11 per cent reduction. This target was weaker even than those of other developed countries – which were themselves insufficient for the action on climate change we so desperately need.

THE NEW CONSENSUS

The year 2016 has begun on precarious economic and political grounds. Snowballing global inequality has led to a demand crisis (a massive shortfall in purchasing power for ordinary families) in much of the developed world. Speed wobbles in the emerging economies, long seen as the last bastions of economic dynamism, are forcing capital to flee to safer havens, especially the real estate of the developed world, which raises the risk of another property bubble. The post-crisis recovery of some of the world's largest economies has been predominantly achieved through accounting tricks and quantitative easing, a practice that consists of printing money and handing it to investment banks for largely speculative ventures. The year 2015 set a new record for mergers and takeovers,[11] indicating that corporate reshuffling, rather than genuinely productive activity, is becoming ever more important for maintaining shareholder profits. Plummeting hydrocarbon prices – as low as US$27 a barrel at the time of writing – are slamming the brakes on expensive and risky extraction techniques for oil and gas, threatening large numbers of jobs in those and related industries.[12] The ideological palace of neoliberalism is crumbling and, despite the chaos, space is opening up for new alternatives. The time is ripe to begin articulating them.

International capital has been organising for this moment, developing instruments to facilitate ongoing profitability amidst ongoing crises. Key amongst these instruments are the free trade and investment agreements, notably the Trans-Pacific Partnership Agreement (TPPA), that are designed to lock in neoliberal policy presumptions and impose heavy financial costs on states seeking alternative approaches.[13] This agreement and others like it provide investors with new rights to challenge and undermine democratically mandated policy decisions, and in doing so to transfer enormous sums of money from public to private hands. This locking-in of private interests is detrimental to action on the environment, as well as a host of other issues.

Resisting these corporate capture mechanisms, which are designed to embed neoliberalism, requires action on two fronts: one disruptive and the other constructive. The first, which is simple and already beginning to take shape, can be summed up in the word 'Blockadia'. This is the international movement that seeks to directly resist and disrupt the infrastructure that locks us into ongoing warming. Many will be familiar with the long-running (and, for now, victorious) battle to stop the Keystone XL pipeline in which indigenous activists, environmentalists, trade unionists, academics and politicians all collectively put their bodies (and criminal records) on the line to disrupt its construction.[14] These long-running acts of organised civil disobedience, combined with the crash in oil prices, have for now halted the project. These actions are already taking place in New Zealand, notably around the Brazilian oil firm Petrobras, which, as a result of a combination of Blockadia strategies, falling oil prices and its own corporate malfeasance, pulled out of its New Zealand deep-sea drilling operations last year.

Governments are only too aware of the effectiveness of these strategies, and our own state has responded by curtailing rights to protest. The urgent enactment of amendments to the Crown Minerals Act (the so-called 'Petrobras law') gave New Zealand's defence forces the power to arrest and detain anti-mining protesters after fisherman Elvis Teddy drove his boat within an exclusion zone to attempt to prevent a Petrobras exploration vessel surveying in the Raukumara Basin. These laws must be resisted as part of the disruptive strategy.

The constructive part of the strategy lies in effective policy-making to directly challenge the primacy of neoliberal doctrine, and I believe there is one key policy that should sit at the forefront of our demands. To challenge the financial controllers of the economy and undermine their monopoly on political power, we must wrest back control over the mechanism of creating money. It is rarely discussed in New Zealand, but private banks have the legal ability to loan out the money they receive in deposits over and over again; and they do so willingly, since not everyone will call in their loans at the same time. This is how most money in New Zealand is generated – it is loaned into existence, with interest charged on top, rather than being created by the Reserve Bank.

If private banks can do it, why not governments? I believe the state should print money to create a large-scale climate jobs programme, funding strategic projects that address fundamental human needs. The policy is not a new one by any stretch of the imagination. Printing money and putting it to work was a core plan of Michael Joseph Savage's post-Depression economic recovery. This money helped create the largest plantation forest in the

Southern Hemisphere, Kaingaroa, as well as wood-processing plants throughout the country that employed thousands of rural workers and created the raw materials for New Zealand's state housing. It is a core plank of the economic agenda of the new British Labour leader, Jeremy Corbyn. He calls it 'quantitative easing for the people'. Many of the world's largest economies, including the United States, the United Kingdom and Japan, are printing money – though unfortunately they typically give that money to large financial houses to gamble on share markets rather than put it to productive use.

This policy is powerful because it strikes at the heart of the neoliberal presumption that the economy should be wholly controlled by private interests, and because it affects the relative affluence of the wealthiest. It rejects the idea that the role of the state in the economy must be minimised if we are to achieve collective prosperity. Most importantly, if the money created in this scheme was used well, to create good jobs that can 'green' the economy, it would counter the myth that environmental action always comes at the expense of the economy – it would, in other words, shatter the false dichotomy between jobs and the environment.

We already know how much of a threat this kind of policy presents to the New Zealand political establishment. In 2012, Green Party co-leader

Russel Norman proposed using quantitative easing to recapitalise the Earthquake Commission after the Christchurch earthquakes had drained its reserves. The policy was met with vitriolic criticism from the political and financial elites, who gave it ridiculous labels such as 'voodoo economics' and characterised Norman as a kind of ecological snake oil salesman. While the policy was pulled from the Green Party's agenda due to internal ructions and the need to undertake political damage control, it is clear that had it not presented such a threat, it would never have been stamped on so emphatically.

We know the ideas are there, it is just that the political will is lacking. We will need to generate that will by coming to terms with ideologically confronting policies and championing them publicly. The links between the economy and the environment must be kept front and centre at all times, and we must build a public consensus that commercial interests have to be put in their correct place – as servants of the planet and people – if we are to halt climate change. If this can be achieved, then the next time leaders meet to decide the fate of the planet, political posturing may for once be replaced by principled decision-making.

5. WELFARE AND PRECARIOUS WORK

CHLOE KING

Politicians often promise my generation that hard work and the right kind of attitude will eventually get us somewhere – somehow, someday. In the meantime we just need to suck it up and endure some hardship on the path to economic stability, the achievement of our dreams and the peace of mind that comes with knowing how we will pay our rent next week. But 'in the meantime' has no end point. There is no certainty as to when the hardship will end and the prosperity will begin. There is no guarantee that economic stability is even attainable for the growing number of young people who feel the choke chain of shrinking pay, reduced opportunity and diminished state support closing around their necks. The young people

I meet often tell me that they are struggling to stay afloat and that it feels as if their options are dwindling. As the welfare state too shrinks, they are left with less and less breathing space if they cannot find employment in a crowded job market or they become too unwell to work and have no wealthy parent to prop them up.

Despite the promises of a 'rock star economy', in 2015 some 64,000 young people were out of work. By another measure, 81,500 were 'NEETs': not in employment, education or training.[1] Up to one-third of workers, including many young people, are in work that is insecure, foisting on them fluctuating start and finish times, little or no guarantee of hours, limited access to benefits like sick leave, and inconsistent paychecks.[2] Increasing numbers of young people, especially those who do not enjoy the benefit of a privileged background, are forced to take any work they can find, no matter how depressing, low-paid, irregular or insecure. This is not the prosperity that was promised. This chapter, then, is about how young people have been lied to. It is a story of how, as governments roll back workers' rights and the welfare state, young people all over Aotearoa/New Zealand, and indeed the rest of the world, are being pushed to breaking point – and how they might start to push back.

HARD WORK DOES NOT MEAN MUCH IN A BROKEN ECONOMY

Charlotte[3] is in her early twenties. Like many others, she has been told that with the right attitude and a bit of hard graft she too can succeed and live 'the sweet life'. The hard reality is that she has rising medical costs, and Work and Income New Zealand (WINZ), the government department supposedly responsible for delivering welfare, has refused to offer any financial assistance to meet them. Charlotte recently suffered a mental breakdown. Because of her mental health issues, which include panic attacks and anxiety, she has had to cut down on her hours at work. She has gone from working three days a week to writing content for an online site when and if she can. 'I have barely eaten and WINZ said they won't give me a food grant. People like me need help.'

Although Charlotte did secure a back payment from WINZ of $130, three weeks without income have left her unable to meet her mounting medical bills, pay rent, buy food or pay back friends who have lent her money. Charlotte told me that she was left without income because there was a two-week waiting list at the WINZ office in her area. Without this appointment she could not get the necessary money from WINZ to visit her GP to gain the medical certificate proving she needed state assistance. In an email, she told me that even after finally gaining the medical certificate she found it hard to access her benefit entitlements, 'I can't get anything I'm entitled to, even though I had all the medical forms and proof.' She went on to say, 'I honestly don't know how to survive this. It makes me feel like there is no point in even trying to get better when just feeding myself is almost impossible. There is no security, it's just endless chaos and stress.' People being denied assistance is a regular occurrence at WINZ according to Auckland Action Against Poverty (AAAP), a beneficiaries' rights group. As AAAP state on their website: 'At least 9 out of every 10 people seen by our advocacy service have been incorrectly or unfairly denied assistance.'

Turmoil and stress are feelings that increasing numbers of young people experience. They are familiar feelings for Missi, a twenty-seven-year-old woman who recently told me she had just been fired from her retail job three days before the end of her ninety-day work trial. The only reason given was that she 'wasn't a good fit'. The power to fire a worker without reason within the first ninety days is a harsh result of the so-called 'Fire at Will' law brought in by the current government. 'I've been laid off four times in eighteen months,' Missi told me. 'I thought I'd have my shit together by now but how can you get ahead if you can't even secure work for longer than a few months at a time?'

Sometimes employers 'fire you before they have to give you any benefits like sick pay or holiday pay. This type of financial insecurity and job loss isn't just depressing: it's nearly pushed me to a full-scale nervous breakdown.' Stuff Media reported in 2014 that, 'A recent study by the workplace firm Regus found 60 per cent of New Zealand respondents were seeing more stress-related illnesses at work, such as headaches and panic attacks. A third said they were having difficulty sleeping because of work worries and a quarter were worried about losing their jobs.'[4] The findings of this study reflect what I hear anecdotally from young people all too often.

In an ideal world, welfare should offer young people like Charlotte and Missi a strong social safety net, so they can refuse work that does not suit their skill-sets or exploits them as workers. In the words of the British geographer Danny Dorling, 'When there is a dole young people do not have to take any work, no matter how bad it is.'[5] But between 2008 and 2014 the Social Development Minister, Paula Bennett, enacted sweeping and punitive welfare reforms which have made going on Jobseeker Support – as the dole is now called – a humiliating and complicated process. The paperwork alone consists of forty-eight pages of forms to fill in. For those struggling with literacy this is yet another barrier to getting financial support.[6] In the year to March 2015, 11,693 people on Jobseeker Support had their assistance cancelled. Of these only 3,489 had found work, shifted to study or otherwise changed status, while 4,916 just dropped out the system because of the paperwork involved.[7] The Labour Party said that people on welfare are losing the paper war.

The idea behind the government's reforms – including the additional hurdles applicants must jump to access support – is that working brings confidence. This is how politicians often justify pushing as many people as possible off welfare and into paid work, regardless of how mentally unwell or physically incapable they may be. But what if the only work you can obtain is part-time and so underpaid and depressing that it erodes self-confidence rather than builds it? When I spoke with Joe Carolan, an organiser from Unite Union, he told me how 'zero-hour contracts and precarious, casualised work is a way for capitalism to mask real unemployment. How many jobs are there where people are just working twelve to fifteen hours in this country?'

Yet we are often told this is the most we can expect in the new economy: casual and zero-hour contracts that offer inconsistent hours and a sense that workers don't matter to their employer. After all, there are hundreds of thousands, if not millions, of economically desperate people lining up at the door willing to work longer hours for less money.

But in the end this does not build confidence. There are only so many times you can be fired with little reason given before it starts to erode your self-esteem and create feelings of shame. And this shame is arguably not an accident but a part of the neoliberal logic of tackling poverty – it occurs by design. If we are all individually responsible for our own desperate and depressing circumstances, if the individual and not the system is at fault, then 'shame' is valid language, a motivating force for people to try harder. Writing in *The Guardian*, George Monbiot explained the logic in this way: 'Kindness is cruelty; cruelty is kindness: this is the core belief of compassionate conservatism. If the state makes excessive provision for the poor, it traps them in a culture of dependency, destroying their self-respect, locking them into unemployment.'[8] Monbiot is referring to the idea of the 'welfare trap'. It is doubtful such a thing exists – and even if it did, far more important still would be the 'precariousness trap' that locks young people into poorly paid, often part-time work with few protections from unscrupulous employers. Even the language used – the 'welfare trap' – is a way of stigmatising (and thus shaming) people who are victims of the system.

The solution for the victims of the system is, of course, the market. In 2015 the government announced that it would pilot social bonds for the welfare system. As the Ministry of Health explained:

Social bonds are an innovative way for Government to contract for social outcomes. Social bonds see private and not-for-profit organisations partner to fund and deliver services to improve social outcomes. If they achieve agreed results Government will pay the investors back their investment plus a return. Investor returns depend on the level of results.[9]

The language of shame is partnered with the language of the market. The belief is that the dynamism of the market is needed to help transform beneficiaries into 'producers', 'consumers' and – best of all – 'entrepreneurs'. Yet if this pilot is fully implemented there will be a financial incentive to bully people such as Charlotte – people who have mental health diagnoses and/or disabilities – into work, no matter how low-paid or unhealthy. Investors make a return only when measurable criteria are met – as when 'x' number of people move into 'y' jobs – but the truly important outcomes, like wellbeing and quality of life, are less quantifiable and so less likely to be addressed. What our most vulnerable people need is compassion, love and support from whatever government is holding power, but the language of compassion and love is one our current ministers do not speak. Instead they speak the language of neoliberalism.

WHAT CONSTRICTED CHOICE LOOKS LIKE

Neoliberalism held out the promise that, once free from state interference, our lives would be transformed and we would have much more autonomy. Once state welfare was abolished, the theory ran, people would be incentivised to find work. If they couldn't, they would be forced to create new work opportunities and undertake jobs that once did not exist. The unemployed would not become unwitting and disempowered victims of the 'welfare trap' because that safety net would simply no longer exist.

The actual result, though, has not been more opportunity, nor an abundance of choice. Instead what many young people have is the illusion of choice, or what I prefer to call constricted choice. This implies very little economic and personal freedom – the two things neoliberalism promised, but failed, to deliver. As a service worker this is what constricted choice looks like for me: I can either pick one meaningless and low-paid bar job with no real guarantee of hours from one week to the next, or I can pick another meaningless, low-paid bar job that perhaps offers more definite hours and benefits such as sick pay – but only, of course, if I can outlast the stand-down period before I am entitled to such benefits. Yet I did what I was told. I got degrees. I worked hard. And like so many other young graduates around the world, I was left with nothing more than limited career options and a student loan I have almost no hope of ever paying back. At times I have worked up to three jobs to scrape together a full-time working week, and I have struggled to find any upward progression or mobility. Throughout 2015 I was working as a bartender and being paid the minimum wage of $14.75 an hour. Just three weeks out from Christmas, I walked into work to discover my shifts had been cut by half with only six days' notice and no explanation given. I tried to choke back my tears as I read the new roster.

When employers can routinely cut your shifts in this way, you face the constant threat of financial ruin, of not being able to pay your bills. Often the cuts are made for trivial reasons, like failing to smile long enough at a customer or not making coffee fast enough.[10] In my experience, not only is this stressful, it also compounds feelings of failure, worthlessness and shame, because no matter how hard I work, I can't seem to get ahead. This sort of job environment also makes workers more compliant. If an employer can cut shifts on a whim, workers have less choice when it comes to reforming their own work environment or even embarking on professional development. We need a campaign which aggressively aims to roll back the use of casual contracts. These types of contracts are largely used within retail and the hospitality sectors and undermine our worker's rights as they offer no guarantee of minimum hours or even a job from one week to the next. Workers deserve to be paid fairly and treated with dignity and respect. This shouldn't be too much to ask.

Other extreme examples of constricted choice are easily found in Aotearoa/New Zealand if you go looking for them. I spoke to a young solo parent who was living in Auckland and working twenty paid hours a week, 'and despite doing everything I was meant to do for WINZ, they cut my benefit and haven't paid me in over two weeks. My current hours don't even cover my rent. I have no money for food, petrol, my power bill is overdue, and I have no phone credit.' When working conditions are deteriorating and the government cuts holes in the safety net, choices can constrict very quickly: 'Lucky for me I can use sex work as a safety net, because WINZ sure doesn't cut it and I would hate to have to work sixty hours in a minimum wage job just to pay the bills – I would never see my son!' This is the reality, the absence of real choice, faced by too many. Choosing between going hungry and taking on dangerous, demeaning, and relentlessly precarious work is not a choice: it is coercion.

All too often, politicians committed to the politics of selfishness tell us that if we refuse to hit the bottom floor and take whatever job is on offer, we deserve everything we *don't* get. But the fact is that the longer you stay in poverty, the harder it is to get out of it. Neoliberalism may argue that our success or failure in life comes down to our 'attitude' and how hard we work to achieve our dreams, while social and economic factors have no real influence on our lives. The myth may be that we make our own luck, that you can make it if you just try hard enough and 'manifest your own destiny'. But there is one word for all of this: bullshit. Changing your attitude is not going to dismantle structural injustice, racism, classism, or sexism, nor will it fix a failed economic model that largely serves the elite. And these myths serve a disturbing purpose. If we struggling young people are told that it is up to us to change our circumstances, if we are encouraged to look inward not outward, we are less likely to rise up and engage in acts of sabotage against the system. If we are too busy trying to change and fix ourselves, we are less likely to demand justice and equality from our world leaders. This self-help language is sold to us as self-empowerment, but mostly it just adds to our growing feelings of shame.

SABOTAGE THE SYSTEM

All over the world, from Aotearoa/New Zealand to North America, models of powerful collective resistance are being built. In our own country Unite Union has waged a decade-long campaign of direct actions, strikes, and protests against zero-hour contracts. The government agreed last year to change the law to crack down on the use of such contracts. However, it was announced early this year that they will be enshrined in law. As workers we know change for the better in our workplaces does not come from politicians or policy makers, it comes from workers who are prepared to stand up together and hit the picket-line and refuse to accept low pay and contracts which undermine their rights. An example was set by the three Wendy's employees who, just before Christmas 2014, walked off the job in a protest against their precarious work. Instead of making burgers for the minimum wage, they made national headlines. Unite also managed to negotiate a ban on zero-hour contracts at other fast food giants such as McDonalds and, more importantly, built an active and informed community to address one of the greatest challenges in the modern workplace. Without that community, which included a diverse range of people from activists to actors, zero-hour contracts would not have been rolled back.

In the United State, the unorthodox 'Fight for $15' movement has won a landmark victory in New York, forcing the state government to lift the minimum wage from $8.75 to $15 – a stunning 70 per cent increase and considerably higher, at current exchange rates, than New Zealand's minimum wage.[11] This victory was meant to be impossible, and it was thought by many that the movement's demand was too great while its organisation was too weak, but in just two-and-a-half years they proved the critics wrong. It helps that the movement's underlying principle is simple and universal: no-one should work and be poor at the same time. Every human being has the basic right to a living wage, to a decent life, and the assurance that the necessities of food, bills, and rent can be paid for with money left over.

It is a principle that partly underpins the work of new collective organisations in Aotearoa/New Zealand like Auckland Action Against Poverty (AAAP), whose followers are becoming well known for disrupting corporate events in order to bring attention to poverty and precarious work in New Zealand. Last year AAAP picketed outside the National Party Christmas function, helped stage a 'hikoi for homes', and even produced important political and economic research. I was at the picket, where for nearly two hours we maintained a hold on the venue and, thanks to this direct action, made national headlines. Some would argue it was a mean-spirited move, but helping change the narrative is all part of disrupting a system which is disempowering and disenfranchising a growing army of young people. We can either go down on our knees or stand on our feet, pushing back against the system and its gatekeepers. I believe that this is how we progress through the interregnum – with collective action. As individuals we face constricted choice, whether in work or in welfare. What we need is change, and that comes only from those who join together to imagine a better world – and then uncompromisingly demand it.

6. RADICAL KAUPAPA MĀORI POLITICS

CARRIE STODDART-SMITH

Having grown up as urban Māori – that is, away from my tribal rohe (area) in a small, predominantly white provincial town – my confidence in distinct or traditional Māori spaces is still developing. I imagine that this is not unusual for those of us who are urbanised and who oscillate between being told that we're too Māori in one world and not Māori enough in the other. It follows from this paradox that, in the words of Māori academic Ani Mikaere, 'what is needed more than anything is courage to question genuinely held but deeply colonised assumptions about what it means to be Māori'.[1] Over the past year or so, I have been questioning what it means to be Māori and whether there is room for a distinctly Māori politics. Having already explored the principles of kaupapa Māori research, this led me to consider how those principles might help inform a kaupapa Māori politics.

Kaupapa Māori is not a new idea or concept. The word kaupapa refers to foundations or first principles.[2] In its contemporary context, kaupapa Māori grew out of a struggle 'with a clear cultural and political intent' to revitalise mātauranga Māori (Māori knowledge) for future generations, and to retrieve space in areas dominated by western discourses.[3] In electoral politics, it re-emerged with the inception of the Māori Party in 2005 and the MANA Movement in 2011. Anecdotally, kaupapa Māori is increasingly referenced as rangatahi (youth) and younger Māori gravitate toward designing their own solutions.

In a broad sense, kaupapa Māori politics is a politics led by Māori, for Māori and with Māori. As kaupapa Māori academic Linda Tuhiwai Smith muses, 'it is what it was, it is what it is, and it will be what it will be'.[4] Similarly, I like to describe kaupapa Māori politics as a lived story. That is, a story that is continuously shaped by our past and our present and that will shape our future. It represents the ongoing story of struggle, resilience and transformation of tangata whenua.

The purpose of this chapter is to present an alternative to the left–right binary that Māori political discourse is often captured within, yet that does not provide the means for understanding Māori dynamics from Māori perspectives. However, before unpacking my narrative it is necessary to first anchor this discussion in its political reality: the annexation of Māori political power.

DISENFRANCHISING TANGATA WHENUA

Following the signing of He Whakaputanga o te Rangatiratanga o Nu Tireni (the Declaration of Independence) in 1835 and the Treaty of Waitangi in 1840, Māori political autonomy was dealt a major blow. Although two versions of the Treaty – Te Tiriti o Waitangi (Te Reo Māori text) and the English text – were distributed for signing, the English version took precedence in the eyes of the migrant settlers, and later their courts, despite the international convention of *contra proferentem* 'which dictates that in cases of ambiguity, a treaty is to be interpreted against the party drafting it'.[5] This is important to note because there are disputes as to what our rangatira (chiefs) who signed the Treaty understood about the document they were signing. Prior to annexation, independent hapū and iwi had for generations regulated the behaviour of their members and determined the terms and conditions on which they were willing to engage in trade and other political activities, as well as the tikanga (customs) through which their rōpu (group) would establish and manage their relationships with tauiwi (non-Māori). However, the seizure of political power and the erosion of rights over our whenua (land) and resources led to Māori disenfranchisement. This was further entrenched by the New Zealand Constitution Act 1852, which denied Māori the ability to share political power.[6] The Act prescribed that only men who held individual title to land had voting rights. But since Māori land was collectively owned, our tūpuna (ancestors) were denied access to political power. This curtailed Māori sovereignty and effectively enshrined Pākehā world views.[7]

Today, Māori political economy remains regulated by the Crown – or, more precisely, by the Crown–Māori relationship which is governed by the principles of the Treaty, defined in the Treaty of Waitangi Act 1975, and refined in 1987 by the 'Lands' case, *New Zealand Maori Council v Attorney-General*, brought before the Court of Appeal.[8]

My worry is that if Māori continue to internalise these principles, to embed them in our own narratives as we have often done, we risk allowing Pākehā interpretations to redefine our relationship with the Crown and its obligations to Māori under Te Tiriti. Ani Mikaere expresses this view when she argues that the Treaty principles do not empower Māori but instead lead to a world in which tino rangatiratanga (sovereignty, autonomy, self-determination) has been sacrificed to the myth of partnership and, ultimately, subordinated to the English-language version of the Treaty text.[9]

Recently, the tensions between tino rangatiratanga and the Treaty principles have emerged through disagreements over the Trans Pacific Partnership Agreement (TPPA). While Māori academics have expressed apprehension over whether the Treaty clause in the TPPA is robust enough to protect Māori rights and interests,[10] the National Government has insisted that the exemption clause is sufficient.[11] Furthermore, in treating the criticism of the clause as trivial through ignoring these concerns, the government invalidates expert Māori opinion and pre-appoints itself as arbiter of Te Tiriti interpretation. It is understandable then that Māori would grab onto the Treaty principles as the only legally recognised means by which the Crown may be held to account – even if only symbolically – to retain a measure of autonomy over the places to which our identities are linked.

Perhaps it is in that spirit that kaupapa Māori scholar Leonie Pihama maintains the Treaty is 'a crucial document which defines the relationship between Māori and the Crown in New Zealand' and 'affirms both the tangata whenua status of whānau, hapū and iwi in New Zealand, and their rights of citizenship'.[12] However, while the principles and the

Treaty have come to symbolise the source of Māori rights, Mikaere argues that 'our rights as tangata whenua of this land' derive in fact from our having been here for generations and 'having developed an intimate connection with this environment, and an intricate set of relationships to regulate our place within it'.[13]

To sum up so far, kaupapa Māori has a difficult relationship to the Treaty. Sometimes it is located in the tradition and politics of the Treaty. Yet it is hard to see how Treaty principles could be foundational to kaupapa Māori when the latter emerged as a resistance strategy, as a 'site for promoting tino rangatiratanga'.[14] Moreover, if our rights as tangata whenua are taken to be located in these documents, this would require us to internalise Pākehā narratives, to adopt them as our own, and, in effect, to ignore the slow erasure of our tino rangatiratanga.[15] Arguably, the Treaty principles cannot underpin kaupapa Māori politics without depriving the latter of its commitment to tino rangatiratanga.

BY, WITH, AND FOR MAORI

Māori Professor Graham Hingangaroa Smith describes kaupapa Māori as the 'philosophy and practice of being Māori'.[16] Others have called it a theory, a methodology and a guiding set of principles.[17] Kaupapa Māori is most often considered in Māori education and research discourses, but it is a philosophy in its own right,[18] comprising a non-exhaustive list of principles with tino rangatiratanga as the ultimate aim.[19]

Kaupapa Māori politics might then be described as a philosophy and a set of practices that are designed, owned, led and delivered by, with and for Māori.[20] The implicit identity requirement suggests a layer of exclusion of non-Māori by unapologetically prioritising the lived experiences and perspectives of Māori. It is about empowering our Māori voices that continue to be silenced by the noise of history, and by the protestations of white New Zealand that insist on shouting us down and shutting us out. Kaupapa Māori politics is intended as a counterweight to the systematic subjugation, denial and attack of Māori knowledge. It is a vehicle for values and identities that potentially overturn Pākehā definitions of 'who we are and our place on our own land'.[21]

The tendency of kaupapa Māori theorists toward strategic essentialism – that is, 'temporarily promoting Māori ethnic/cultural identity [to] achieve certain political and social goals' – is, as Māori academic Te Kawehau Hoskins explains, necessary but should not become orthodoxy.[22] After all, kaupapa Māori politics does not prohibit Pākehā from engaging with it. Instead, it encourages those engaging with Māori to adopt a kaupapa Māori approach to ensure they are personally and culturally equipped for that engagement. For instance, when a researcher or politician is developing a policy for Māori, it asks that they examine their own experiences and biases, and consider 'what they bring with them' that is of positive benefit for Māori on a personal level. On a cultural level it asks what they know about the experiences and aspirations of the Māori community they hope will benefit from the policy.[23]

When kaupapa Māori begins to produce positive outcomes for Māori through the development of culturally responsive and relevant social and economic policy, the exclusionary layer linked to identity dissolves. This derives from the central importance of whānau in te ao Māori (the Māori world) and the 'responsibility to nurture and care for relationships (manaakitanga)', to recognise and uphold the mana (respect, integrity) of each person, and to extend aroha (love, respect) to ensure that all people, Māori and tauiwi (non-Māori) alike, are cared for.[24] Kaupapa Māori politics, then, is inherently geared toward inclusiveness even though tauiwi are transitorily excluded. Through the process of whakawhanaungatanga (the building of rapport and getting to know each other), inclusiveness is reinforced and a policy space emerges in which everyone benefits.[25] This is because aroha is viewed as paramount in building and maintaining relationships, and is considered a 'prerequisite for the possibility of any productive social or political alliance'.[26] However, in order to ensure kaupapa Māori politics is productive, Māori epistemologies must be positioned as starting points, not reduced to cultural notions that are benchmarked against western assumptions.[27]

THE RADICAL POTENTIAL OF KAUPAPA MĀORI POLITICS

A key principle of kaupapa Māori is the concept of ako Māori, which acknowledges both the philosophies and practices that are inherent and unique to Māori *and* those that 'may not be traditionally derived but are preferred by Māori'.[28] This means that different western ideas may complement the diverse perspectives of kaupapa Māori frameworks, but it would be an error to construe such ideas as essential to them. Many Māori drive a socialist agenda, for example, and although there are commonalities with some aspects of tikanga Māori, socialism as a political philosophy should not be seen to be implied by Māori narratives.

The radical potential for kaupapa Māori politics lies precisely in its ability to transform and engage with other theories while retaining its distinctively Māori core. Indeed there is a form of anarchism known as 'mutualism', that I believe would be an appropriate complement to kaupapa Māori in its struggle to retrieve policy space and reclaim our tino rangatiratanga. This is not to suggest that mutualism is the *only* possible complement to kaupapa Māori. The connections between these traditions have not yet been sufficiently explored, even though they might avoid the contradictions between kaupapa Māori and the legalism of the Treaty tradition.

In the words of mutualist Kevin Carson, mutualism favours 'an evolutionary approach to creating a new society' and 'emphasises the importance of peaceful activity in building alternative social institutions within the existing society', thus rendering the current statist system obsolete.[29] Similarly, kia piki ake i ngā raruraru o te kainga, the kaupapa Māori principle of socio-economic mediation, emphasises the need to assist in the 'alleviation of negative pressures and disadvantages experienced by Māori communities'.[30] Whānau Ora, kura kaupapa and kōhanga reo are examples of kaupapa Māori initiatives that Māori have used to alleviate distress and deprivation while building our own culturally relevant institutions.

Mutualists base their property rights on 'personal occupancy and use'.[31] This concept is similar to ahi-kā-roa, in which hapū would customarily 'keep the fires burning' to show that they had occupancy and use of a particular site and its associated resources. Mutualists also support 'a society in which all relationships and transactions are non-coercive, and based on voluntary cooperation, free exchange, or mutual aid'.[32] An historical example of this is the signing of Te Tiriti o Waitangi, which demonstrates that independent iwi and hapū were willing to co-operate with the Crown and its subjects for the benefit of both parties. The agreement was that Māori would retain control over their lands, resources and tikanga, and in return the British would be entitled to settle peacefully and manage their citizens in accordance with their own laws.[33] This illustrates the pragmatism to which Māori societies were inclined.

Another commonality is that mutualists, like kaupapa Māori advocates, are critical of the co-option of language and ideas that advance the agendas of statist regimes. For example, mutualists consider markets to be 'a profoundly humanising and liberating concept' but oppose the way markets have been 'co-opted and corrupted by state capitalism'.[34] Likewise, kaupapa Māori advocates condemn the way that colonisation embedded patriarchy in tikanga Māori, distorting the importance of mana wahine in pre-contact Māori society.[35]

The co-opting of ideas and language also

feeds into what are arguably misconceptions of collectivism imposed on, and internalised by, Māori. Māori society is often described as inherently collectivist. I do not dispute the idea of collectives, but the way this term has come to be understood and applied to Māori frameworks leads us perilously toward a view that Māori society is homogenous. Certainly, Māori society is built on smaller collectives, but these resemble co-operatives in which the members, through a shared whakapapa (genealogy), collaborate to achieve the aspirations of their rōpu. It is not like the homogenised collectivism of statism, which threatens to ignore the diversity of tikanga within and between whānau, hapū and iwi.[36]

Mutualism also emphasises flexibility around collectivism, focusing on small-scale co-operatives and engaging in mass collective action only when required.[37] This has its parallel in the kotahitanga movement, which speaks to the value of unity and solidarity. Generations of Māori have demonstrated that solidarity is necessary in struggles against mass repression. The foreshore and seabed hikoi in 2004 was a modern example of collective action through kotahitanga. But kotahitanga should not be confused with solidarity under the banner of the state. As Māori jurist Sir Eddie Durie argues, 'Māori customary opinion is antithetical to the concept of the state.'[38] Moreover, Māori 'eschew a universal superordinate authority and centralised controls, preferring instead a plurality of dynamic authorities'.[39] Similarly, Māori writer Ross Himona denounces the way that Pākehā interpretations of Māori histories create hierarchies within whānau, hapū, and iwi, failing to take into account the complex relationships that exist within and between these collectives.[40] The importing of hierarchies into Māori thought and practice is also noted by Ani Mikaere, who suggests that the task remains to 'disentangle these colonised notions' from our tikanga.[41]

Internalising the collectivism of statism is also dangerous because it leads us to erroneous conclusions about ourselves. By casting Māori as a homogenous national collective, and establishing the idea of 'them and us' in hierarchical opposition, the state was able to disenfranchise Māori communities, and the effects persist to this day.[42] In my view, a national Māori collective that is wedded to the state is the antithesis of kaupapa Māori. This kind of relationship inherently subordinates tino rangatiratanga and prioritises the agenda of the dominant power – the state – thereby reinforcing oppositional hierarchies built on assumptions of white supremacy.[43] This is counter-productive in the struggle for the redistribution of political power. The complement of mutualism, however, enables Māori to reach into non-traditional spaces without subverting tino rangatiratanga, as happens in statist systems.

WEAVING THE PAST AND THE PRESENT INTO OUR FUTURE

We must recognise that hierarchies and collectivisms entangled in, or imposed on, Māori discourses come not only from those who are overtly trying to undermine kaupapa Māori. They also spill from the narratives adopted by supposedly political allies. An example presented itself during the 2014 general election, when the leader of the Labour Party, David Cunliffe, claimed that 'Labour [is] *the* Māori party'.[44] His reasons boiled down to having fourteen Māori candidates and a manifesto underpinned by the Treaty partnership.[45] Previously, Cunliffe had suggested poverty was a characteristic of being Māori when he insisted that Māori disproportionately benefit from Labour Party policy.[46]

These incidents indicate the ongoing colonisation of our political identities and the silent assumption of Māori homogeneity. Lurking here is also a preoccupation with 'deficit thinking' – that is, the widely prevalent view that the disproportionate representation of Māori as disadvantaged on socio-economic indicators is not because of negative life circumstances but because being Māori is a deficiency. This model influences both how the public view Māori and also how we see ourselves, because it presents a distorted view 'of Māori as simply failing', and in the process denies the existence and experiences of Māori who are succeeding.[47] To overcome this deficit thinking, we must assert the right to not be constrained by the left–right dichotomy. We should instead embrace the co-operative practices of our tūpuna as a means to reclaim policy space and the right of Māori to lead on Māori solutions.

One of the obvious challenges for Māori is reconciling kia piki ake i ngā raruraru o te kainga with tino rangatiratanga. As mentioned earlier, Māori are adept pragmatists, capable of operating inside the system to alleviate the immediate stress and pressures on whānau and working outside it to build alternative social institutions. Both approaches enable the transformation to self-determining whānau and hapori Māori (Māori communities). Mutualists would object to the idea of working within government to achieve social transformation. But as an indigenous people whose political power has been actively and aggressively seized, and who continue to battle the trauma of colonisation, Māori must be free to change the framework on both fronts. A purely oppositional stance can become a prison. Admittedly, kaupapa Māori theory has 'strategically promoted forms of cultural essentialism and oppositional political stances/analyses' and those stances have been useful for rights recognition, but, as Hoskins argues, we must move from 'opposition to' toward 'responsibility for' others. This is consistent with the centrality of whānau in kaupapa Māori philosophy.[48] If Māori remain confined to an oppositional stance, we will impose ideological constraints upon ourselves and destroy the transformative potential of kaupapa Māori.[49]

There will never be just one type of kaupapa Māori politics because, as mentioned above, Māori are not the homogenous ethnic cluster portrayed by much of the media and indeed the public. Māori society has always been divided and dynamic; this is reflected in the way that we collectively organised ourselves into hapū and, later, iwi, as a way of differentiating ourselves and our claims on resources. As Māori legal academic Māmari Stephens writes, we can see that division and dynamism in our deepest histories – for example, in the stories of 'Tāne separating Rangi and Papa in the face of opposition from Tāwhirimatea [or] Māui's enduring conflicts and collaborations with his brothers in fishing up Aotearoa and slowing Tama-Nui-te-Rā'.[50]

Like mutualism, kaupapa Māori encourages us to envision a utopia but to be realistic about what we can achieve at each step.[51] The transformation will not be won through adversarial, mana-diminishing politicking, or through ideologies that are complicit in suffocating our voices, but through respecting the mana of others and extending aroha without expectation. Kaupapa Māori is not socialism or capitalism, nor is it left, right or centre, because it does not sit beneath the cloak of a western ideology. Although it may be complemented by such theories, it is designed by, for and with Māori – though also for the benefit of all. The strength of kaupapa Māori is that it is an idea in motion, weaving its way through time and space, responding to different environments and contexts, perpetually subject to individual and collective shaping.

Kaupapa Māori emerged to resist the political subjugation of Māori, but it is not the preserve of one party or rōpu. To ensure that kaupapa Māori retains its distinctively Māori core we must actively prevent Pākehā narratives from wilting our commitment to retrieve political space. This is the only way we will dismantle the vestiges of colonisation, transform how we interact in a multicultural society, become the architects of our own solutions, and counteract the unequal distribution of power in Aotearoa/New Zealand.

I leave you with the words of esteemed iwi and community leader Rangimarie Naida Glavish: 'Tū Māori mai' – stand as Māori.

7. CONTRIBUTING TO PUBLIC LIFE FROM AFAR

LAMIA IMAM

In the Chinese zodiac calendar, 2016 is the Year of the Monkey. I myself was born in the Year of the Rat, or, as I like to call it, the Year of the Peter Dunne. The Honourable Peter Dunne entered Parliament about five weeks after I was born in the Christchurch Women's Hospital. Mine was not an overly political household, but politics has become so much a part of my life that I have taken to measuring time according to years served by our elected members.

My identity is inescapably defined by my life experience. I was born into a Bangladeshi Muslim family while my father was on a scholarship at Lincoln University; I then left New Zealand when I was a toddler, and spent my childhood and teenage years in Bangladesh and the United States respectively. I did not come back to New Zealand until I decided to go to Canterbury University. These three nations, their political systems and their cultures have hugely shaped my values.

I have struggled to maintain connection with 'home' for as long as I can remember. When we first arrived in Bangladesh I was just three years old, and, according to my mother, I begged to go back home – home being Christchurch. But when our family moved to the United States, I yearned to return to Bangladesh from this place where the language, food, clothes and customs all seemed so alien.

I was in high school in a small town in midwest America when 9/11 happened. My family is relatively devout, but that was the first time I had ever heard the word jihad. There were only three Muslim students in my little high school; in the days after the attacks we were interviewed and assured that we would not face racism. The opposite was true: I had to deal with racism then, and have dealt with it ever since.

When I finally came back to New Zealand years later, I knew I had found home. The thing I remember most fondly is how friendly and welcoming the customs and immigration officer was. 'Welcome home,' he said to me after looking at my New Zealand passport; I was happier than I had ever been in an airport. That was the first time someone made me feel like I was at a place that was mine. Everywhere else I was an outsider or a foreigner. Now, I find myself back as a guest in the United States, where I am quite literally an alien. But being away from home is very different in 2015. Now we have Skype and Facebook and Twitter; home is just a snapchat away.

Thanks to my global upbringing, I lack a Kiwi accent. And so I am confronted with ignorant opinions from people like the broadcaster Paul Henry, who notoriously claimed that Sir Anand Satyanand, then the Governor-General, did not 'look and sound' like a 'Kiwi' owing to his lack of a Kiwi accent and his Fijian-Indian heritage. By Henry's logic, I am probably unqualified to be Governor-General. While I am indeed unqualified to be Governor-General, I would hope that it is not because of the way I look or sound.

Contributing to New Zealand politics via the public media of Twitter and blogging, I find myself having to frequently defend my Kiwi credentials. 'I was born in Christchurch!' I exclaim, while listing all the 'Kiwi' things that I love. The Pākehā culture of New Zealand is both accessible and exclusive. On the one hand it is everywhere, dominant and ever-present, but it is also restrictive. People who do not look and sound Kiwi are supposed to do whatever they can to be as Kiwi as possible and then they can have admittance to the club. Immigrants are expected to adopt New Zealand's language, culture and customs, and forget their background – or else be forced to hear that well-worn line, 'If you love your culture so much, why don't you go back to where you came from?' This is not a hypothetical fear. I have frequently been challenged this way in person and online, as retribution for daring to talk about my cultural or religious values. This is the bind: you have to assimilate to be accepted, but you are not accepted because you are still a different-looking person with a funny-sounding name. And a major double standard is at play. When expat Kiwis in Hong Kong or London form social groups around their shared language and culture, it is not frowned upon. But when expat South Asians or Arabs do the same they are seen to be rejecting the idea of being Kiwi. We should be trying harder to 'assimilate' – with a group of people who are openly hostile to the things that make us who we are.

One of the most frustrating questions I regularly face, no matter where I go, is: 'Where are you from?' Whether I am online dating, walking into a job interview, or meeting new people socially, people are very curious about my ethnic origins. Most people, faced with that question, can state their hometown and move on, but I do not have a 'hometown', and my assertion that I am from New Zealand is generally not accepted straight away.

'But what is your ethnic origin?' 'But where were your parents born?' 'But you don't have a Kiwi accent?' 'But Lamia is not a Kiwi name?' These are follow-up questions I face. When I explain my background, the usual conclusion is, 'Oh, so you are Bangladeshi! That makes sense.'

My immediate family do not live in New Zealand. They chose to emigrate to the United States. I have extended family in Finland, the Middle East and Australia. I am not 'just a Bangladeshi', in a globalised world, but is anybody really just one nationality? Many Bangladeshis would frown upon my lifestyle, my life decisions and my political values. I find myself frowning upon *their* lifestyle and political values: as a progressive feminist, I have views on marriage and religion that are unconventional by Bangladeshi standards. I have a hard time identifying with many aspects of Bangladeshi culture because I was not brought up in that environment. Boxing me into an ethnicity just because it is difficult to accept that a globalised world has led to a global culture may be a coping mechanism for a lot of people, but it fails to deal with the reality of diversity, which is always complicated and multidimensional.

CHOOSING NEW ZEALAND
For many personal reasons, I have chosen New Zealand as my home. The most frustrating aspect of

this decision is the fact that other people think they have the right to relitigate and remake it for me. One reason I identify as a Kiwi is New Zealand's politics. While I was in graduate school in Texas, my peers often made fun of me for my 'socialist' perspectives on policy-making. There are differences between the political left and right in New Zealand, but there are also certain values that Kiwis share – and in the United States these are often labelled 'radical'.

The need for a public health system is perhaps the most striking example. In 2005, I was in a major car crash while travelling from Christchurch to Nelson; my medical bill was $0. I should note that I did not have medical insurance. I am grateful that I happened to be living in New Zealand at the time. I am grateful that an accident has not burdened me with a lifetime of debt. I am happy that I had the opportunity to pay into an ACC system that both afforded me that health care and ensured that other Kiwis could have the same access. I chose New Zealand not just because it chose me through accident of birth but also because it most closely resembles the kind of society I want to be part of.

I have spent my whole life connecting to New Zealand from the outside, even when I was inside the country. Despite being from birth a New Zealand citizen, I was denied a Kiwi upbringing because my parents were not themselves citizens.

Later, my accent and ethnicity meant I was not accepted as a Kiwi when I began my adult life here as a student. But I am still, as I said, a New Zealand citizen, thanks to having been born here before 2005, and I am glad of that fact.[1] Our little country is not perfect, but it has made enormous strides in many areas throughout its history, and has created institutions – such as ACC – that are world-renowned. It has at least attempted to create a partnership with its indigenous people through Te Tiriti o Waitangi. It does not shy away from asserting its values on the world stage. It has been led by women in its executive, legislative and judicial branches of government. These policies and this approach to governance are what makes it easy for me to choose New Zealand as a home.

And yet … even when I was physically in the country, working at Parliament and then later at the Office of Treaty Settlements, I felt I was an outsider. New Zealand tends to clump all minorities in one box and ignore the realities of certain privileges. Being of South Asian heritage is decidedly not the same as being tangata whenua. Being a cis woman is vastly different from being a trans woman with a disability.[2] Being a heterosexual woman of colour is radically different from being a white gay man. In some respects, I represent the majority – but I am hyper-aware of my privilege because in other respects I am the minority. In the last two years,

I have reverted to being an outsider by choosing to pursue higher education and greater work experience in the United States, so that I might one day come back and contribute to New Zealand society in a better way than if I had stayed. I go to great lengths to maintain my connection with New Zealand. My family, who now live permanently in the United States, would love me to make Texas my home. Wages in the United States are much higher and that in itself is a compelling reason; but the politics make choosing Texas difficult. So I continue to comment on New Zealand politics and social issues by Tweeting and blogging, because I am committed to staying connected to my home and these platforms provide that opportunity.

And yet ... I recall standing in line to pay tuition fees at Canterbury and being yelled at by the woman behind the counter for not standing in the International Students line. She had no way of knowing by looking at me that I was a New Zealand citizen. I felt humiliated because I was not given the opportunity to defend myself while all the other students assumed I was a confused foreigner. When I finally walked up to the counter and explained quietly that I was a New Zealand citizen, the woman's embarrassment was not enough vindication for me. I felt publicly disgraced and I wanted to tell every student who heard and saw the incident that I had a right to stand in that line. In another instance, I was volunteering at the Canterbury Community Law Centre and a highly distressed client started screaming at me about immigrants, and specifically Muslims, taking over the country and ruining his job prospects. Even when I was trying to 'integrate' by getting an education and giving back to the community, acceptance was hard to come by. Contributing to New Zealand society from the outside is not a new experience for me even though it is only now that I am physically far away from it.

CONNECTING TO NEW ZEALAND

My experience is no different to that of many minority ethnic people living in the developed (white) world. Our parents or our grandparents emigrated to countries like the United States, the United Kingdom, Canada, Australia and New Zealand, and to European and Asian countries, in order to give their children a better life. We in turn try to challenge their belief systems and the societal norms within which we are forced to exist. In our parents' world we are defiant, too westernised, and devoid of faith and a sense of duty. In our own society, we are prudes, we have strange eating habits, we steal jobs, and we have tendencies towards terrorism. And yet my identity isn't just my skin colour or religion. I was a political staffer (and I continue to live and breathe politics); I am a woman of colour; I am a blogger; I am a progressive feminist.

Ordinary Kiwis supposedly do not care about identity politics, which suggests to me that they don't have an identity. The current narrative separates identity from politics when they are in fact intertwined. Are there no hard-working, tax-paying lesbian Kiwis wanting to own a house? Are there no Kiwi mum and dads raising a transgender child? Are there no Māori women wanting equal pay? Are there no hard-working Kiwis with family members in the criminal justice system? The welfare system? The health system? Identity provides a unique perspective on the problems faced by Kiwis. When identity is removed from these issues we do not get the full picture. The term social justice is supposed to represent the intersection of identity with government policies. Some of these policies, which disproportionally exclude certain people with a specific identity from having the life that all Kiwis seek, can only be critiqued from the perspective of someone with that identity. For example, we assume that everyone has equal access to our public health care system but it is clear that trans people do not. There are not enough doctors to cater to their unique needs and when concerns are raised, those concerns are dismissed because trans health care is seen as an identity politics issue rather than a health care issue. We also seem not to have any space for intersectional feminism; indeed it is often derided as 'identity politics', something that doesn't fall into the category of 'real issues'. I am not the only person who is an outsider because of my accent and skin colour. The culture of our society designates people as outsiders so their voices can be lawfully excluded and marginalised. This happens when we give more credence to privileged groups and by default silence the less privileged.

I take to social media to dispel some of the myths about people like me, but also to submit an alternative voice to the current narrative. Much has been said about 'social justice warriors' on social media. They are mostly denigrated by self-proclaimed thought leaders, pundits, commentators, and even journalists. It is unclear if these groups resist alternative views because citizen-initiated investigations and political blogging are an encroachment on their work or because they view discussions regarding social justice on social media as ineffective. But politicians, journalists, and other powerful entities are on social media, and so it provides an opportunity to influence debate in a way that has never been available to advocates of social justice previously. I should note that I do not believe I make a material difference by being on Twitter or by blogging my ideas. What I do believe is that I am bearing witness. I do not want future generations to ask, 'Why did you not speak up?' and I believe I can get my voice heard better on Twitter than on the steps of Parliament, although the effect will not likely be seen for quite some time.

Traditional methods of activism are not necessarily applicable in the twenty-first century. Social media has allowed me to connect to 'home' from the outside and continue to be part of a new form of political conversation. On the one hand, social media is dismissed as a bubble, an inconsequential medium. But often it is also cited as the source of opinions, thoughts, an indicator of public sentiment. This Schrödinger's social media, which is simultaneously trivial and significant, is often the only way that previously marginalised groups can get their voices heard. It is unsurprising to me that this very fact might make many people and institutions nervous. We as a society do not have a good history of including marginalised voices in decision-making at the highest level. When politicians talk about 'welfare reform', how often do they consult women, the largest group of recipients because of historical exclusion from the workforce, childbearing and rearing responsibilities and other reasons? When we talk about 'racism', how often do we bring racial minorities onto a TV panel? When we talk trans health care, how often do we actually talk to trans men and women? How often do we dismiss issues that affect actual people's lives as not 'real'? These issues, combined with the enormous economic and environmental burdens we face, mean that our generation faces an incredible uphill battle. We may not be able to afford to buy our first home, we are burdened by more debt than our parents ever were, we are living under mass surveillance with our every selfie and sexy email potentially tracked, and we are tasked with the enormous responsibility of dealing with climate change and instability around the world.

But in New Zealand at least, we still have a chance of forging a better future. In 2004, just five months after I had moved to New Zealand as an adult, the foreshore and seabed hikoi culminated in front of Parliament. I confess I had no idea what it meant or what the issues were. But I remember that when I visited Parliament for the first time in 2009, as part of my political science studies, the openness and accessibility of the institution and the politicians shocked me immensely. And just two years later I was working there. I believe that there is no other country in the world where I could have been able to get where I did. Americans firmly believe in 'American exceptionalism', their assumed role of being an exemplar to the rest of the world. In New Zealand, in contrast, we have the 'tall poppy syndrome' – and because of that we forget how exceptional we truly are. If my travels and studies around the world have taught me anything, it is that New Zealand has just as much of a chance to be a leader now on issues such as the refugees crisis and climate change as it did in 1984 when it decided to take a stance on nuclear weapons.

What New Zealand needs is continued engagement, whether it is through hikoi to Parliament or through social media. Instead of getting bogged down in frustration because we are not achieving progress at the rate we want, we have to keep engaging. That is why I continue to connect with New Zealand through blogging and social media. During the 2011 election, I was working for Labour leader Phil Goff. Our central election issue was asset sales. About a week after the election, during a meeting, our correspondence person read out a letter asking whether we were aware that the government planned to sell off state assets and what Labour planned to do about it. We had spent the entire election campaign – every speech, every television ad, and every social media post – telling the public about Labour's opposition to asset sales, and still we did not get that message to every voting person. That was one of the harshest and most jarring moments of my working life.

I was born in the Year of the Peter Dunne, but I was also born in the year of New Zealand declaring itself a Nuclear-Free Zone. I choose New Zealand as my home because its people and its society have the kind of values I have. People knowingly make certain decisions, but they make many political decisions because they are misinformed. My hope is that perseverance can change that. I dream about evidence-based policies and rigorous public debates, and New Zealand is small enough for us to make those things happen. I want to be a part of that conversation and I want to be a part of that future.

8. FEMINISM AND SILENCE

HOLLY WALKER

When I was an MP, I used to tell people that I went into politics to use my voice. Yet at the end of three years in Parliament, I had lost my voice completely.

When I found out I was pregnant in early January 2013, I was full of hope and excitement, about both the new life growing inside me and the possibility of being a mother in Parliament. I felt strongly that women should be able to combine parenting with politics, and I was looking forward to showing that it could be done.

A few others, like Ruth Richardson, Whetu Tirikatene-Sullivan, Katherine Rich and my contemporary Nanaia Mahuta had done it before, and it seemed like each trailblazer had made it a little easier for those coming next. Parliament's Speaker, David Carter, granted me fourteen weeks' parental leave and, for the first few months after my return, the ability to go home at 6 p.m. instead of working until 10 p.m. My Green Party colleagues arranged to cover my portfolios while I was away and keep some of my workload after my return so that I could ease back in. My partner took time off from his job as a manager at the Waitangi Tribunal to look after our daughter full-time.

People kept sharing photos of an Italian European Parliament member, Licia Ronzulli, to my Facebook timeline. These showed her daughter growing from a newborn to a toddler on her lap while her mother voted in the chamber. Though I didn't plan to take my baby into the House with me – with a parents' room across the hall where I could breastfeed, it didn't seem necessary – I expected to seamlessly integrate a small person into my busy professional life. I probably hoped people would send articles about me to each other in a few years' time.

I was used to functioning highly, packing a lot into my days, excelling at everything I tried. I assumed that combining parenting and politics would be no different.

I was wrong.

In the months after I returned to work, those images of Licia Ronzulli began to haunt me. They just didn't compute. There was no way my kid would have slept peacefully in my arms if I had tried to take her into the debating chamber. She would have screamed the House down with reflux and vomited on my papers. She certainly disrupted many Green Party caucus meetings this way. Each morning it felt like I was tearing myself in half leaving her, even though my partner brought her in for a feed at lunchtime. I left caucus and select committee meetings at regular intervals to express milk, and found myself with an out-of-control oversupply problem (don't ask). She was not a 'good sleeper'. My nights were spent in a kind of half-life, wedged in the crack between my bed and her cot. I was chronically sleep-deprived and increasingly anxious. I checked myself against an online post-natal depression scale and got a score that I didn't want to think about.

Then my partner developed chronic pain as a result of a neuromuscular disorder, and things really turned to custard. For most people, being an MP is actually a two-person job: partners provide a huge amount of behind-the-scenes support. When my partner was suddenly unable to support me, let alone take care of our baby, it became clear that we had officially moved from 'just coping' to 'not coping'. Something had to change.

In July 2014 I announced I would relinquish my place on the Green Party list. The relief that came with letting go of the job was palpable. Yet I couldn't shake the feeling that I *should* have been able to do it. Maybe if my family hadn't suffered a tragedy in 2012 that called on me to provide a lot of support. Maybe if I hadn't had a baby so soon after becoming an MP. Maybe if Dave hadn't got sick.

Maybe if I was a man.

In the wake of my departure I was asked a lot of questions about whether my experience showed that it was too hard for women to have babies in Parliament. For reasons that I couldn't articulate at the time, it seemed important to emphasise that there were no structural barriers. I wanted people to know that I had simply experienced a particularly difficult run of bad luck. Others could – and should, I insisted – do it in my wake.

And yet.

WITHDRAWING FROM PUBLIC LIFE

When I was still pregnant I had invited Katherine Rich up to my office for a coffee.

I didn't know her well. In the early 2000s, when she was a National list MP based in Dunedin, I had teased her on the pages of the Otago University student magazine I edited for misspelling coconut as 'cocunt' in a recipe she had sent through at my request, instead of correcting it as a more mature person would have done. She wasn't very happy.

In 2012 I had a Members' Bill pulled from the

ballot that would have introduced a lobbying disclosure regime to New Zealand politics. I invited prominent lobbyists – Rich, in her role as chief executive of the Food and Grocery Council, among them – to meet with me to discuss how the bill might affect them. Our conversation was amicable.

So when I fell pregnant, I felt as if I could approach her to pick her brains about what it had been like to become a mother in Parliament. She was generous, honest and encouraging, though perhaps for my sake she held back a little on the difficult reality. At the end of our conversation she said something that struck me as strange at the time. 'If you ever need anything,' she said, 'even just someone to stand in your office and hold your baby while you work, I would do that for you.'

This was a woman I barely knew; a woman I had once ridiculed, a lobbyist I was trying to regulate, and a former MP from the opposite end of the political spectrum; a woman who was very busy with her own job and family. Yet in that moment, she was simply a mother offering support to another mother. I'll never forget it. Now, I think that offer was Rich's way of telling me that she knew how hard it would be. Parliament is not an easy place for women, let alone new mothers.

Looking back, there are ways I felt silenced by Parliament right from the beginning. When I delivered my maiden speech, my usually strong and confident voice threatened not to come out at all, so daunted was I by the occasion and the place.

In the first few months, I was often required to speak on bills I knew nothing about. The days were so full, I would have only a few minutes to frantically scan a bill before delivering the Green Party's position. Once, late at night, faced with a particularly obscure heritage bill, I begged the colleague who had held the portfolio before me to give my speech, certain I would otherwise crash and burn. She generously obliged, even though she also had her own bills to cover. It was a stunt I could pull only once.

Gradually, as I listened to the quality of debate in the House, I realised that aside from ministers and one or two subject experts, most MPs knew very little about the bills they were speaking on. Most simply riffed off one or two talking points to fill their ten minutes. Knowing this, I got better at thinking on my feet, but I never shook the feeling that my utterances were not worth recording as a legally admissible part of Parliament's proceedings.

Select committees, too, were impenetrable. I was late to my very first meeting (I got lost), and was gently ridiculed by my fellow members, who had already elected the chair and vice-chair. Committees rely on punctual attendance to retain finely balanced majorities. Had the committee's decision not been pre-ordained by Parliament's

Business Committee – the weekly meeting of the Speaker and party whips that decides much behind closed doors – I could have been in big trouble.

Thereafter I was on the back foot, scrabbling to access papers on the electronic filing system, decisions whizzing past me before I'd had a chance to figure out if I had anything to say. Items of business were dispatched at a bewildering pace, and though I had strong opinions and pertinent questions to ask, I often missed the opportunity to voice them because of my uncertainty about when it was okay to speak. Again, I got better at this, but I was never completely comfortable.

On social media, too, my voice diminished. I had joined Facebook and Twitter long before becoming an MP and was comfortable sharing compromising photos and strong opinions with an audience of friends. Yet as my personal social media accounts morphed into political profiles with official authorisations, my ability to share my true thoughts diminished. I could no longer fire off a tweet full of feminist rage and swear words without the risk of reading about it in the *Dominion Post* the next morning. I learned to self-censor, a habit that has been hard to unlearn. Even now it's not unusual for me to write and re-write a 140 character message for ten minutes before abandoning it, worried about what people will think.

When I had finally discharged my responsibilities

in the 2014 election campaign, I turned off my already diminished voice altogether. I drew the metaphorical duvet over my head. I hated it when people asked me about politics, Parliament or my experience. I developed a fear of public speaking and a phobia of situations where people looked at me to lead. Gradually, I withdrew from every other position of authority I held – community boards, committees, my local Green Party branch – the lot. I found a fulfilling new job with no public-facing aspects, and kept my head down.

TRANSFORMING PUBLIC LIFE

Slowly, as I recovered from the bruising experience of discovering my own limitations, my perspective on what had happened started to change. As I looked around me at friends, colleagues, fellow parents, and family members, I realised that everyone was carrying heavy burdens. My hard three years did not set me apart – they made me like everyone else.

Contending with grief and loss, balancing work obligations with care responsibilities, caring for children, providing emotional support to loved ones – these are what make us human. Rather than wishing that they hadn't happened to me so that I could have stayed in Parliament, I started to wish that our democracy could be more accommodating of our humanity, of our limitations.

The courageous women who recently stood up in Parliament to disclose their histories of sexual and physical abuse, and to demand an apology from the Prime Minister for trivialising rape, powerfully demonstrated that MPs carry heavy burdens too. Like everyone else, MPs are complicated, damaged humans. But Parliament is not an easy place to express your full humanity.

As the Green Party's electoral reform spokesperson, I spent a lot of time thinking about MMP. The introduction of a proportional voting system in 1996 saw a rapid improvement in the percentage of women in Parliament, one of the strong arguments for retaining MMP at the 2011 referendum.

Yet after leaping from 21 per cent in 1993 to over 29 per cent in 1996, the proportion of women in Parliament has remained largely static for the last twenty years. Many politicians and academics have debated how to resolve this. Most of the solutions proffered encourage more individual women to put themselves forward, and challenge political parties to identify and foster more women candidates. To their credit, most parties are attempting to do this.

Ultimately, though, this approach requires individuals to put themselves and their families through the wringer of an election campaign and then, if successful, to subsume themselves to the sometimes absurd demands of a parliamentary career. For me, these included working from (at least) 8 a.m. until 10 p.m. on sitting days; a punishing travel schedule; nights and weekends full of public events; being expected to accept phone calls from journalists at any time; conversations about welfare policy at the supermarket; bruising encounters in Question Time; being shouted at by angry members of the public; and having my body and clothes criticised online.

Sure, the pay's pretty good, but everyone knows what it is, and they won't let you forget that you'd better work hard to earn it. The subtext is: if you can't handle the heat, get out of the kitchen. But what if, instead of waiting for people to burn out and get out, we threw open a few windows and doors and tried to bring the temperature in the kitchen down a few degrees?

Until we figure out how to do this, I don't think Parliament will achieve gender equality, let alone welcome the more diverse voices of those with different abilities, ethnic backgrounds and gender and sexual identities.

I've got a few ideas about where to start, although this is just a personal wish list that needs to be part of a wider conversation.

We have a list-based political system. Why not let an MP take an unpaid leave of absence for a year, to be temporarily replaced by the next person on the list? This would allow a more manageable early parenting experience, while also providing invaluable training for up-and-coming politicians. The same provision could also be used by MPs needing to care for sick relatives or recover from illness.

Could electorate MPs run on a joint ticket and job-share? I ran a joint campaign in Lower Hutt with another candidate. We stood for adjacent seats, although she actually lived in the same electorate as me. She has four children; I had a new baby and a sick partner. We are both highly capable, articulate women with a lot to offer but also a lot of care responsibilities. The Green Party only elects list MPs, but theoretically, if a job-share was available, I'm confident we would have been fantastic.

Can we review the days and hours that Parliament sits to make them more family-friendly? Late nights are difficult for Wellington-based MPs with small children, and so is spending thirty-plus weeks away from home for parents from other electorates. What if Parliament sat for fewer weeks in the year, five days a week, finishing at 5 p.m.? The same number of constituency days could be preserved, parents could spend more weeks at home, and those whose children are with them in Wellington could spend the evenings with their family.

What about the draft code of conduct for MPs that's been floating around for years but going nowhere because the major parties refuse to sign it? Is it really too much to stipulate that it's not okay to shout people down when they are speaking, make rape jokes in committee meetings, or comment on a woman's body hair in the lunch line? (All of these are real examples, by the way.)

Such behaviour notwithstanding, can we also reject the stereotype of sleazy, venal politicians? I know that some seem to go out of their way to justify it, but most are genuine individuals drawn by a strong set of values to a career of public service. Let's see them as humans first, and politicians second.

Beyond Parliament itself, I think what we need is really the project of this book writ large. Let's unstitch the neoliberal, individualistic mindset we've all internalised and work on building community and connection again.

Until recently, I was as guilty of it as anyone. I am a product of neoliberalism and – despite a precarious start – a privileged upbringing. I was born in 1982. My childhood took place against a backdrop of radical economic reform and the growth of the cult of the individual. Yet I got the start in life I needed – and that every child deserves – thanks to the vestiges of collectivism. Due to a last-minute marriage malfunction, my mum found herself nine months pregnant with no house, no job, no tertiary qualification and no husband. She found a council flat, signed up for the DPB, and accessed the Training Incentive Allowance to train as a kindergarten teacher. By the time I was seven, she was teaching full-time and had met and bought a house with a lovely man who became my dad. Meanwhile I was already showing the signs of being a precocious over-achiever, thanks to my public education. The remainder of my childhood was thoroughly middle-class, filled with ballet recitals, skiing holidays and baby siblings. I thrived, winning every prize going at school, flying through music and dance exams, performing in amateur dramatics and developing a taste for debating and politics that was eventually to lead me – via a Rhodes Scholarship – to Parliament.

Somewhere along the way, I started to feel like if I could do it, anyone could.

It's such a dangerous narrative. It's so easily twisted to justify strict welfare reform, privatisation of collective assets and greater 'choice' in education and social housing. Prominent New Zealanders with similar trajectories, who went from receiving state support to positions of national leadership, use this narrative of private achievement to justify pulling the ladder up behind them. But it's wrong. To borrow from my former colleague Russel Norman, stories like these don't mean that a state house kid, or a public school kid, or a DPB mum can do anything. They mean that the state's commitment of collective resources to housing, education and income support really does make a difference.

It's this that I think we need to relearn. The value of collectivism. The power of community.

Max Harris calls it the politics of love in the final chapter of this volume. I think that's right, but it's not enough to ask individual politicians to espouse it. We need to think about how to remake our democracy and our institutions to enable it.

RETURNING TO PUBLIC LIFE

As for me, and my voice, I'm pleased to say I found it again. I spent a year reading only words written by women. Intuitively, I knew that writing might be a safe way to use my voice again, but I needed to digest lots of examples of women doing it before I could figure out what I wanted to say.

I took an online writing course and met a group of fierce women on the other side of the world who I could safely share all of myself with, precisely because they knew nothing about me or my thwarted political career. I practised on them, and slowly, tentatively, I started sharing pieces like this one.

These days, I have no desire to resurrect my political career, at least not in the foreseeable future. But now that I have found my voice again, I have every intention of using it.

9. RELIGION AND THE REAL WORLD

DANIEL KLEINSMAN

When Pope Leo XIII released a document in 1891 reaffirming the rights of workers to unionise and managers to own private property, he was condemned by both socialists and capitalists alike. When Pope John XXIII released a document in 1963 demanding a better commitment to human rights, secular leaders offered a similar rebuke. What did religious leaders know about the secular? Popes were not authorities on politics and economics, the critics said, and they should confine themselves to the strictly religious. The criticisms may sound familiar because they are nearly identical to those Pope Francis faced after publishing *Laudato si': On Care for Our Common Home,* a Papal encyclical urging the world to take immediate and comprehensive action against climate change.[1] But the question remains: does a pope's 'apostolic exhortation' have any weight or relevance in the modern world? Pope Francis may have found favour with the left after calling for political as well as social and economic change, but many others maintain that religious leaders should not mix their religion with on the 'real world'.

Yet this is precisely what Pope Francis is inviting us to consider: the real world, where – quoting New Zealand's Catholic bishops – he says that 'twenty percent of the world's population consumes resources at a rate that robs the poor nations and future generations of what they need to survive' and where runaway climate change threatens even humanity at large.[2] Francis calls on all the people of the world to take 'swift and unified global action' to combat the problem. This call to act against climate change and social devastation is not new, but the particular manner in which Francis calls us to act certainly is. Francis urges us to navigate and appreciate the challenging reality of climate change within a framework of relationships and interdependence: taking action, in his view, is the responsibility of neither religious nor social institutions in isolation; it is a political task for the community at large.

If we are to 'restore the various levels of ecological equilibrium', writes Francis, we must '[establish] harmony within ourselves, with others, with nature and other living creatures, and with God'.[3] In other words, our relationships with each other and with nature give rise to a responsibility to act. Significantly, and perhaps surprisingly, Francis goes on to speak not of a conversion to Christianity but rather an 'ecological conversion' and a 'community conversation'. This conversion and conversation must include everyone 'according to his or her own culture, experience, involvements and talents'. Such a conclusion is not necessarily religious; if anything it is an argument for democratic realism. It urges us not to obscure the world and its issues with exclusive ideologies or individual interests, nor reduce it through relativism (or an equally reductive absolutism). Instead we must encounter the world and the crisis of climate change as it is. Of course, the Pope is quick to conclude that such an encounter reveals social and environmental devastation that demands an urgent response.

But the question then becomes: what kind of approach is appropriate in Aotearoa/New Zealand? Our country comprises many different cultures, interests and perspectives, and we celebrate and draw strength from this. But we also suffer from escalating social unrest, increasing imprisonment and growing levels of poverty. This indicates that progress is failing to include everyone. The lesson from Francis is not to look at each issue in isolation but to treat the bonds between concern for nature, justice for the poor, commitment to society and interior peace as inseparable. 'Environmental deterioration and human and ethical degradation are closely linked.'[4] We see this when, for example, the expansion of business districts deprives people – including those who now sleep on the streets in these areas – of land that could otherwise serve their basic needs. Thus, any reluctance to care for our beautiful country, and any tendency to see it in terms of our individual interests, is inseparable from a reluctance to care for our fellow human beings. Refusing to see the world within a framework of relationships reflects a tendency to see others as merely objects of, or obstacles to, our individual interests.

THE CRY OF THE EARTH AND THE CRY OF THE POOR

This is the Pope's innovation: the insight that no relationship exists in isolation, that 'a true ecological approach always becomes a social approach; it must integrate questions of justice in debates on the environment, so as to hear both the cry of the earth and the cry of the poor.'[5] Francis acknowledges early on in his document that 'realities are more important than ideas' and, consistent with this approach, he accepts that 'the Church has no reason to offer a definitive opinion.'

He hastens to add, however, that we need only take a frank look at the facts to see that our common home is falling into serious disrepair. That is the reality.

Of course, if we isolate issues and compart-mentalise our concerns, anything that doesn't directly affect those specifics or serve our immediate interests becomes irrelevant. Francis speaks of this as a practical relativism, or a fragmentation of information, which quickly becomes a form of ignorance. He talks also of a tendency to see creation as merely a collection of materials to be manipulated and exploited, and he calls this a technocratic paradigm. We approach problems as technical difficulties to be corrected according to this paradigm, and ecological values are reduced to various marketing measures. Talk of sustainable growth 'usually becomes a way of distracting attention and offering excuses', as when oil companies refer to economic and employment opportunities in developing countries as factors in favour of further exploitation.[6] When the environment is mentioned, it is considered within this dubious context of 'sustainable growth', even though further exploitation for the sake of short-term economic gain can come only at the overall expense of developing countries and their environments.

This technocratic paradigm teaches us to be

attentive to that and only that which demands our attention, namely the market. We deify the market and make ourselves subject to its forces. We even personify it with language like 'jittery' or 'temperamental' in market analyses, as if it somehow has the power or personality to produce an economy worthy of humanity. Meanwhile, we talk of the environment and society as cold bodies of facts, or objects of utility, and we consider the impacts on these as collateral damage – as if nature and other people are something external to us. But this is to deny our interconnected reality and, in the end, to deny our human dignity. According to Francis, 'when human beings fail to find their true place in this world, they misunderstand themselves and end up acting against themselves.'[7] Thus he claims that '[i]t cannot be maintained that empirical science provides a complete explanation', and he calls for an 'openness to categories which transcend the language of mathematics and biology, and take us to the heart of what it is to be human'.[8] It is not that Francis opposes science or technology; indeed he celebrates these things as 'wonderful products of a God-given human creativity' and recognises that, by informing our understanding of our world, they 'produce important means of improving the quality of human life'. The science of quantum physics reflects our interconnectedness, while the science of evolution illustrates the awe-inspiring intricacies of creation, culminating in the mystery of human consciousness, to take two examples. Francis simply requests that room be left for aesthetic sensibility, poetry, philosophy and religion in an effort 'to grasp the ultimate meaning and purpose of things'.[9]

This kind of aesthetic and philosophical approach invites us to eschew the cold and remote logic of the market and to recognise that 'solutions will not emerge from just one way of interpreting and transforming reality'. Instead we must appreciate 'the various cultural riches of different peoples, their art and poetry, their interior life and spirituality'. Taken seriously, such recognition and respect prevents one from reducing reality to 'us versus them'; it also prevents a religious reduction to black-and-white absolutism. In an exhortation of 2013, Francis warned that 'a supposed soundness of doctrine or discipline leads ... to a narcissistic and authoritarian elitism.'[10] Such elitism leads, in turn, to what Francis calls 'distorted anthropocentrism', a mode of thinking that he says characterises the current ecological crisis. It also leads to the polarisation that dominates the politics of climate change: we converge in two opposing camps according to our immediate interests and associations, and are generally unmoved by the concerns or considerations of those outside that immediate sphere.

REALISING THE VISION

But how do we show respect for the various cultural riches, concerns and considerations of other people while doing justice to the integrity of our own cultural identity? We do so by way of relationships. It is within this framework that Francis offers his perspective which is inspiring beyond the limitations specific to his particular cultural identity. This is what *Laudato si'* offers us: a human truth and a human solution. Francis's encyclical transcends itself: it is not merely a religious perspective on climate change but also a perspective shared with the purpose of engaging others and generating a widespread conversation. It is a commentary on the very nature and future of human progress. It is something that transcends the tired binaries of black and white, right and wrong, religious and secular, and instead offers us a new vision for the world. This vision values religion as a mode of interpreting the meaning of life, but not to the exclusion of alternative insights. It is a vision of democracy in the deepest sense of the word, one in which religion doesn't reign as ideology but remains relevant within a framework of relationships.

Laudato si', then, is about interconnectedness. This is how Francis presents both his religious convictions and his sense of the wider world – as an interconnected reality. The two things are mutually inclusive because they are both about relationships and realising humanity. The creation stories of the Bible attempt to illustrate this human truth. In the Garden of Eden, harmony was lost when Adam and Eve presumed to take the place of God – when, that is, they refused to acknowledge their human limitations and denied their relationship with the rest of creation, including the environment. In the story of Cain and Abel, harmony was lost when Cain denied his duty to love and to care for his brother – when, that is, he became envious, denied his relationship with his brother and committed the ultimate injustice against him. In the story of Noah and the Ark, harmony was lost when people disregarded the rhythms inscribed in nature, including those in themselves; renewal came about by recovering these rhythms and restoring a relationship with all of creation, including themselves. From this Francis concludes that 'when all these relationships are neglected ... life itself is endangered.'[11] 'These ancient stories', he adds, 'bear witness to a conviction which we today share, that everything is interconnected, and that genuine care for our own lives and our relationships with nature is inseparable from fraternity, justice and faithfulness to others.'[12]

It must be said that in these stories and laws as Francis articulates them, there is an emphasis on male-dominated language that is unhelpful (particularly in the context of a document dedicated to relationships and inclusiveness). Rather than focus on the singular, however, we must recognise that each perspective contributes to the greater whole – and indeed depends on other perspectives to properly realise that whole. Francis's perspective, limited as it is, need only inspire us to respond and to partake in what he calls the 'conversation which includes everyone'. Thus, we can extend and amend these illustrations in terms of our own cultural riches, concerns and considerations. What is required of us is that we 'take into account the nature of each being and of its mutual connection in an ordered system' and recognise that 'the Spirit of life dwells in every living creature and calls us to enter into relationship with [them].'[13]

This also offers an antidote to the fundamentalist approach that projects preconceived ideas and expectations about sexuality onto others, rather than taking into account their nature and encountering them as they are. A true relationship with God, neighbour and earth means not purporting to be the arbiters of what is worthy of our recognition and respect and what is not. It also means not pretending to be the authors of our own good fortune, nor presuming that any opportunity we have is one to which we are entitled. We can extend these illustrations beyond the language limitations of Christianity, changing the stories to suit other cultural perspectives.

TO WHAT END, IN WHAT NAME?

In Aotearoa/New Zealand we prioritise independence and opportunity, we celebrate equality and we defend freedom as the absence of intervention. We are taught that the only obstacle to our own success is ourselves. The problem is that, in truth, the equation for what we might call 'success' invariably involves many factors other than ourselves – in particular, other human beings and other living things. To those who say they are the authors of their own success, that everyone enjoys equal opportunities and some people simply do more with theirs, it might be said: look around you, extend the opportunity-cost-analysis beyond yourself, and see the people who are without precisely that which you possess. Or as Francis might put it, encounter the world as it is.

Equality is a peculiar concept. It is impossible to define how different people might be equal, yet the intuitive belief in equality is one of our most strongly held convictions in Aotearoa/New Zealand. The problem is that this belief is used to deny diversity and disregard the different demands that come with this reality. It is used to deny our duty to our neighbour and to deny our relationship with others. And this destines us for an individualism and isolation in light of which the word 'equality' itself loses meaning. We say, 'Equality means no special treatment', as if responding to the particular needs of another threatens the fulfillment of our own needs or the realisation of our own equal dignity. Francis wants us to realise precisely that the other's needs are inseparable from our own and that the other's welfare is interdependent with our own.

So we must recover the meaning of this word equality. I suggest that it is not so much a reality to be celebrated as an ideal to be pursued, a call for each of us to participate in the whole by investing in all other parts (of which the whole consists). This is what Francis refers to when he talks of an 'integral ecology', one marked by a broader vision and a capacity for living together in communion. The phrase 'the whole is greater than the parts' does not mean that some parts are greater than others, nor that the more powerful majority is greater than the minority, but rather that each part is an essential component of the whole. In this sense we are already equal. This view assumes both autonomy and interdependence within relationships. For without autonomy an individual contribution cannot be made to the whole and our greater reality cannot be realised, while without interdependence autonomy becomes either isolated and impotent, or disordered and destructive. Francis observes in this regard that 'the external deserts in the world are growing, because the internal deserts have become so vast'.[14]

A modern response to this reality of relationships depends quite simply on change. To engage with interconnectedness in a meaningful way, we need to be converted. To hear both the cry of the earth and the cry of the poor we need a conversion experience that inspires action. Naomi Klein, reflecting on her experience at a Vatican conference on climate change, refers to conversion and the Church's belief in people's capacity for change when she says, '*[I]f* transformation is as contagious as it seems to be here [in the Vatican] – well, we might just stand a chance of tackling climate change.'[15] But to inspire action requires more than just pointing to relationships or interconnectedness. The reality of the greater whole is only compelling in the presence of a new narrative. Francis suggests a new narrative that focuses on beauty: '[b]y learning to see and appreciate beauty, we learn to reject self-interested pragmatism.'[16]

Yet the problem is that the traditional religious story is incompatible with our complex cultural context; it is, in the words of the Catholic priest Thomas Berry, dysfunctional in our modern-day reality. In Aotearoa/New Zealand our new narrative must recognise the Treaty of Waitangi and, as Tony Spelman suggests, our identity as either tangata whenua or tangata tiriti. This means that tangata tiriti, as the beneficiaries of the Treaty, must not pretend to be, or act as, the sole benefactors or sole trustees of the estate of Aotearoa/New Zealand. Nor should they purport to be the arbiters of what is in the interests of the country and its people. Such an ignorant and arrogant approach neglects the reality of interdependence, a reality on which the Treaty was founded and our future rests. Our narrative must acknowledge our national history, inconvenient and uncomfortable though that may be, because it is part of how we came to be and part of the context within which we must build our future. Our shared identity must also be broad enough so as not to exclude those beyond our borders because, for tangata tiriti, the right of access to this country existed only by virtue of such an inclusive perspective on the part of tangata whenua.

Beyond this, however, I find myself unable to be any more definitive without reducing or obscuring our reality, as Francis warns against. This, I think, reflects the fact that an individual can only really talk about what we need to talk about, which is a start. However, the realisation of a shared identity and story, and a solution, comes about only by way of a conversation that truly includes everyone. It is not a matter of simply changing the language or even transforming the power dynamic. Individualistic thinking cannot solve the problems of individualism. The task, therefore, is not to devise an abstract notion of identity or an abstract solution. Rather we must be much more aware of, and attentive to, the rest of creation as much more than a collection of materials or objects of our interests.

The starting point is a new narrative and renewed relationships, from which – as Francis says – 'a new social fabric emerges. … [This cultivates] a shared identity, with a story which can be remembered and handed on.'[17] Within this context, religion can be seen as a vital thread of the social fabric, in which leaders and thinkers from Francis to Spelman have something important to offer. These leaders draw us into the community experience and call forth a dynamic, participatory response, so that their role as leaders is one of inspiration rather than instruction, and our response is – for each of us – our own to be realised and related. When, and only when, this is realised and related by all will we realise the vision of the greater whole.

10. THE POLITICS OF LOVE
MAX HARRIS

When we debate the future of Aotearoa/New Zealand as a community, we need healthy criticism of the current state of politics and society. But we also need to fix our minds on how our country could be better.

We need concrete policy proposals that can achieve structural change. We need fresh ways of thinking about politics and people. Just as much as we need a root-and-branch review of where we are going, we need seeds of hope to be planted – and new water for our collective garden.

Here I set out one positive proposal, one seed of hope, that might sustain that garden: the politics of love.[1] But what is the politics of love? How is it grounded in values and inspired by Māori ways of thinking? And how might it work in a messy world of different concepts, ruthless politics and difficult trade-offs?

The politics of love is particularly important in Aotearoa/New Zealand today for two reasons. First, words matter, and the politics of love can refresh the stale language of our present-day political sphere. Second, we live in an 'age of loneliness',[2] and the politics of love has the potential to provide the solidarity, warmth and support that so many seek – including those who suffer from solitude through unemployment, old age, mental health difficulties or incarceration.

WHAT IS LOVE – AND WHAT IS THE POLITICS OF LOVE?

Love means different things to different people. We have varied experiences of it, in families and friendships and society. But we can, perhaps, agree that at its core it is a feeling of deep warmth that is directed outwards towards an object, such as another person.[3]

What else can we say about love? First, it is not a static state. It is transmitted or expressed, often in an active way through words ('I love you'), gestures (a kiss, for instance) or other actions (such as through gifting). Because it is beamed in this way from one person to someone or something else, the idea of love is closely tied to relationships and the connections between people.

Second, there is a depth to love. Love is not a superficial feeling; it has heft and gravity. The words 'I love you' are not said lightly in a relationship; we associate love with 'heart' for this reason. Love is a feeling that accumulates over time or over the course of experience.

Third, love is not based only on reciprocity. It can be responsive to other acts of love, or appreciative of something or someone else. But it is closely tied to kindness and generosity in that it involves a certain selflessness or virtue. The Māori term aroha, which is often translated as 'love', is defined by Cleve Barlow as 'an all-encompassing quality of goodness'.[4]

So if this is love – a feeling of deep warmth that is directed outwards, often in an active way, and closely tied to relationships and selflessness – what shape would the politics of love take?

The politics of love is possible only in a world where politics is driven by values – aspirational principles for good conduct that are less cold, and perhaps more soft-edged, than 'ethics', and which may be best summed up by the Māori word kaupapa. Philip McKibbin and I have suggested elsewhere that the New Zealand public may be hungry for a values-based approach at a time when politics appears to be dirty and politicians seem distant from the realities of everyday life.[5] Some values, like 'fairness' and 'opportunity', are often invoked in electoral politics in Aotearoa/New Zealand, but others (including kindness) are seldom cited. Some may feel that these latter values are too precious and too likely to be tarnished in the rough-and-tumble of political life, but in my view they will stand up to the test – and we cannot do without them.

I propose that we make love the key value in the practice of our politics. A politics of love is a politics motivated *by* love. It requires politicians to enter Parliament for generous reasons. It calls on them to search their consciences to ensure that they are driven not by self-interest or financial gain but by selflessness, relationships, and love. (I do not mean to suggest that all politicians are motivated by self-interest and financial gain, only to call attention to those motives wherever they are.) And it involves different policies than those currently pursued. It may require a more humane approach to prisoners, a willingness to accept a greater number of refugees, and a less mean-spirited attitude towards those receiving welfare benefits. But politics is of course broader than this – it relates to the proper exercise of power anywhere in society. A fuller treatment of the politics of love might also consider how it could transform, among other things, the family, the interactions between friends, and activism.

BACKGROUND TO THE POLITICS OF LOVE –
AND SOME COUNTER-ARGUMENTS

Philip McKibbin and I are by no means the first to explore the idea of the politics of love. The American writer bell hooks has developed the concept at length.[6] Politicians such as former United States President Jimmy Carter and Czechoslovakian President Václav Havel have referred to love. The philosopher Martha Nussbaum calls for 'civic love' in her book *Political Emotions: Why Love Matters for Justice*.[7] Closer to home, Andrew Dean in *Ruth, Roger, and Me* has argued that the feelings of discomfort and disconnection felt by many New Zealanders must be answered by aroha.[8]

But the politics of love is not without its detractors, and several criticisms deserve a careful response.

First, why 'love'? Why not some other value or ethical precept, like 'dignity' or 'compassion' or 'respect'?[9] The answer to this question, in the main, is that love has a meaning that is distinct from these other terms; 'dignity', 'compassion' and 'respect' are not synonymous with love, even if there is some overlap in meaning. Love is less cold than 'dignity' or 'respect', more closely associated with selflessness than either of these values, and requires more active engagement than 'compassion'. Love also has the appeal of being tied to everyday life to a greater extent than values like 'dignity', 'compassion', or 'respect', which have a more rarefied air.

Second, it has been said that politics is too brutal and cut throat for love.[10] Love would have to be diluted to accommodate modern politics, this line of reasoning goes, or politics would have to be transformed beyond what we can imagine to accommodate love. It is true that politics today can be vicious, petty, and unprincipled. But it has not always been this way. Humans have in the past endeavoured to construct new visions of politics, and could do so again in future. Indeed, the gap between what people want from politics today – to be listened to, to hear debate on matters of principle, to achieve long-lasting change – and what people often see in politics – partisan bickering, personal attacks, greed, narcissism, detachment – is further evidence of the need for fresh values, including love, to be introduced.

Third, some argue that politics always requires trade-offs, and that we would need to weigh the demands of love against competing concerns such as efficiency.[11] This is a fair point, and it is always difficult to incorporate the more idealistic elements of political theory into the gritty, imperfect policy-making process. In the end, we can only call for those trade-offs to be carried out in a thoughtful and evidence-based way, and for the value of love to be given specific consideration in that process.

That conclusion may be disappointing to some. But it is important to recognise that many goals need to be pursued in modern-day politics. Love is but one value, albeit a value of particular importance.

HOW THE POLITICS OF LOVE COULD REFRESH POLITICAL LANGUAGE AND ADDRESS LONELINESS

The language of politics today lacks clarity and the capacity to inspire. The academic Jane Kelsey has described how neoliberal ideology and policy have produced language that hides the harmful effects of political reforms. Unemployment has been described as 'shedding workers', she notes, a phrase that implies that workers are dead skin rather than living and breathing human beings. Meanwhile, 'broadening the tax base' is the favoured euphemism for transferring the tax burden from the wealthy to the poor.[12]

More generally, the vocabulary of most mainstream politicians is stale and sterile, the values tired, the statements half-hearted. Our Prime Minister, John Key, the leader of the country and the figure whom we might expect to be most visionary and most statesperson-like, exemplifies this trend. A glance at his speeches from the first half of 2015 reveals that certain stock phrases emerge again and again. New Zealand is in 'good shape', he said on 28 January in a speech on social housing;[13] the term 'good shape' was used again on 14 April in a pre-Budget speech to Business New Zealand.[14] The Prime Minister's speech on 2 July to the Canterbury Employers' Chamber of Commerce deployed more stodgy adjectives: he talked of 'tough decisions', 'significant progress', 'strong leadership', and 'solid economic growth'.[15]

On particularly momentous occasions, such as Waitangi Day and the Anzac commemorations at Chunuk Bair in April, he has showed a little more colour.[16] But in general his speeches rely on uninspiring physical metaphors – 'good shape', and the need to 'knuckle down', as he said to the Dubai Chamber of Commerce on 26 April[17] – or technocratic language. He typically speaks in the language of a 'careful and balanced economic programme',[18] or a 'consistent programme of sensible economic reform'.[19]

To be fair to John Key, many politicians across the English-speaking world are equally uninspiring; and Key's language reflects a deliberate decision to eschew grand oratory, since his own skills lie elsewhere and his image – a key part of National's success – is one of moderate, careful leadership. But words still matter. They reflect a politician's vision of politics – and the words Key chooses imply a sadly stunted vision of politics as little more than technocratic corporate management. There is no clear sense of what is valuable to the Prime Minister, beyond being 'careful' or 'balanced'. It is not obvious, either, what it means for the country to be in 'good shape': or in what respect we might be said to be doing well.

The politics of love could help reinvigorate the language of New Zealand politics – and provide a deeper, more substantive standard for what it means for the country to be in 'good shape'. There are other values that could be invoked more frequently in New Zealand politics, like reconciliation, and kindness, and community; the politics of love cannot do all this work of refreshing politics alone. But it is not a stretch to suggest that it might inject some imagination and depth into a policy-making environment that represents a failure of imagination in so many fields. The politics of love could express a new relationship between citizens (so often coldly called 'consti-tuents') and the servant-leaders meant to represent them. It could remind us all that Aotearoa/ New Zealand is a country, not a company – with identities and emotions and all the ups and downs of human life.

As well as refreshing political language and thought, the politics of love might help fill a social need for solidarity, companionship and community. *Guardian* columnist George Monbiot has suggested that we live in 'an age of loneliness'.[20] Although humans were 'social creatures from the start', in England today young people face an 'epidemic' of loneliness, and more than 1.2 million men over the age of 50 claim to have a moderate to high degree of social isolation.[21] Television is the principal companion for many, Monbiot says, and we may be entering a 'post-social condition'. Moreover, '[W]e live in a culture where it's increasingly difficult to find ways to connect for free.'[22]

The age of loneliness is not confined to England. According to the 2010 New Zealand Social Survey, one in three adult New Zealanders say they have felt lonely in the previous four weeks. Some 18 per cent of young people feel lonely all, most, or some of the time, compared to 11 per cent of elderly people.[23] The survey notes that both poor mental health and lower economic standards of living are associated with increased loneliness.[24] Women are more likely to feel lonely than men.[25] (No data is presented on whether loneliness is greater for Māori as opposed to non-Māori.) Those who have not had face-to-face contact with friends or family in the last week are more likely to feel lonely, as are those who have been discriminated against in midlife.[26] (The data has not, at the time of writing, been updated to take into account surging social media use since 2010, and may underestimate loneliness rates by generally focusing on New Zealanders over the age of 15.) Further research is needed on the risks of loneliness, but there is at least anecdotal evidence, and a theoretical possibility, that loneliness is at the heart of some of the harms involved in unemployment and imprisonment, as well as being a proximate cause of some criminal offending.

Loneliness has deep, complicated, structural causes that cannot be remedied solely through a few passing references to love in political settings. But a thoroughgoing politics of love, one which involves not just rhetorical shifts but also changes in policy and the motivation of politicians, could begin to address the epidemic of loneliness that is faced by young people, the elderly, those with mental health difficulties, some of those who are unemployed, many of those who are incarcerated, and perhaps all those who are excluded from society.

The mere expression of the politics of love could hearten those who feel lonely; it could send a message to them that they are not alone and not ignored. Policies flowing from the politics of love – which could include renewed support for prisoner rehabilitation and refugee resettlement programmes, increased investment in sport and general community organisations, and the strengthening of services such as Lifeline and the Samaritans – might address loneliness even more directly. Put simply: love, and a politics of love, could be the answer – or part of the answer – to loneliness.

CONCLUSION

So what is to be done by those committed to the politics of love? What actions can you take once you finish this book and walk away?

Activist movements can continue to use the language of love in protest, submissions, and advocacy. Love is already a common theme in many campaigns; in Aotearoa/New Zealand, #legaliselove was the hashtag and key slogan for some groups lobbying for marriage equality. And in 2015 the line 'love not hate' was all over placards at British protests calling for a more pro-refugee government policy. Politicians might invoke the word more frequently as well. The Green Party hinted at the politics of love in their 2011 campaign message, 'Love New Zealand', and such references could be more explicit. Politicians, many of whom do have good intentions, might also reflect on their motivation for being in Parliament.

Ultimately the aim could be to make love a national value. It is arguable that humility already has that status. 'Kāore te kumara e kōrero mō tōna ake reka' is an oft-heard Māori proverb or whakatauki: 'the kumara does not speak of its sweetness'. One of our most famous citizens, Sir Edmund Hillary, demonstrated such humility in his modest reaction to being the first person ever to climb Mount Everest. Brendan McCullum strengthened the status of humility in his leadership of the Black Caps at the 2015 Cricket World Cup, often downplaying his personal achievements and emphasising the importance of collective endeavour.

In the same spirit, could love be a value that Aotearoa/New Zealand becomes known for, in our politics as in other walks of life? This would undoubtedly require a transformation in how we do politics and how our politicians see us as citizens. But maybe, just maybe, this is a transformation that we are all ready to fight for. Aroha mai, aroha atu. Let's get started.

NOTES

Chapter 1

1   Radio New Zealand, 'Organisers: TPP protests biggest NZ has seen since 1981', http://www.radionz.co.nz/audio/player/201788169 (accessed 5 February 2016).

2   Bill Rosenberg, 'Issues In Privatisation – Costs and Benefits', paper presented at Fabian Society Seminar: 'Are There Any New Arguments For Privatisation?', Wellington, 6 October 2010.

3   Max Rashbrooke, *Wealth and New Zealand*, Bridget Williams Books, Wellington, 2015.

4   'Oxfam says wealth of richest 1% equal to other 99%', BBC News, 18 January 2016, http://www.bbc.com/news/business-35339475 (accessed 25 January 2016).

5   See the Employment Contracts Act 1991 and Budget 1991.

6   Vernon Small, 'David Parker stresses egalitarian roots', Stuff, 5 July 2014, http://www.stuff.co.nz/national/politics/10236591/David-Parker-stresses-egalitarian-roots (accessed 20 December 2015).

7   United Nations, 'Policies for Inclusive and Balanced Growth', 2012, http://unctad.org/en/PublicationsLibrary/tdr2012_en.pdf (accessed 20 December 2015).

8   'Child Poverty Rates in New Zealand are on the Rise', The Wireless, 15 December 2015, http://thewireless.co.nz/articles/child-poverty-rates-in-nz-are-on-the-rise (accessed 20 December 2015).

9   Brian Easton, 'An Egalitarian Society?', Briefing Papers, 6 October 2015, http://briefingpapers.co.nz/2015/10/an-egalitarian-society/ (accessed 20 December 2015).

10 Karl Marx and Friedrich Engels, *The Communist Manifesto*, ch. 1.

11 Timothy Shenk, 'Booked #3: What Exactly Is Neoliberalism?', Dissent, 2 April 2015, https://www.dissentmagazine.org/blog/booked-3-what-exactly-is-neoliberalism-wendy-brown-undoing-the-demos (accessed 20 January 2016).

12 Jane Kelsey, *The FIRE Economy*, Bridget Williams

Books, Wellington, 2015, p. 126.

Chapter 2

1   Alison Flood, 'Eleanor Catton Blasts Critics' "Jingoistic National Tantrum"', *Guardian*, 30 January 2015; The Guardian Online, http://www.theguardian.com/books/2015/jan/30/eleanor-catton-blasts-critics-jingoistic-national-tantrum (accessed 23 August 2015).

2   Ibid.

3   Radio Live, 'Sean Plunket: Eleanor Catton a "Traitor"', 28 January 2015, http://www.radiolive.co.nz/Sean-Plunket-Eleanor-Catton-a-traitor/tabid/506/articleID/69858/Default.aspx (accessed 23 August 2015).

4   Dan Satherly, 'John Key: I'm Not "Profit-Crazed"', Newshub, 28 January 2015, http://www.3news.co.nz/nznews/john-key-im-not-profit-crazed-2015012810#axzz3QJBYXPQP (accessed 23 August 2015).

5   Michael Field, 'Eleanor Catton's Problem with NZ,' Stuff, 28 January 2015, http://www.stuff.co.nz/entertainment/books/65463098/eleanor-cattons-problem-with-new-zealand (accessed 23 August 2015).

6   RadioLive, 'Eleanor Catton's Father and Sean Plunket Discuss Intellectualism in NZ,' 30 January 2015, http://www.radiolive.co.nz/AUDIO-Eleanor-Cattons-father-and-Sean-Plunket-discuss-intellectualism-in-NZ/tabid/506/articleID/70038/Default.aspx (accessed 23 August 2015).

7   Philip Catton, 'On Some Qualities of Respect', The Pantograph Punch, http://pantograph-punch.com/post/on-some-qualities-of-respect (accessed 23 August 2015).

8   Field, 'Eleanor Catton's Problem with NZ.'

9   Michael J. Sandel, *What Money Can't Buy : The Moral Limits of Markets*, Penguin Books, London, 2013, p.48.

10   David Harvey, *A Brief History of Neoliberalism*, Oxford University Press, Oxford, 2007, p.8.

11   Jane Kelsey, *The FIRE Economy*, Bridget Williams Books, Wellington, 2015, p. 179.

12   Jane Kelsey, *Reclaiming the Future: New Zealand and the Global Economy*, 2nd edn, Bridget Williams Books, Wellington, 1999, p.8.

13   RadioLive, 'Intellectualism in NZ.'

14   Ibid.

15   Catton, 'Respect.'

16   'Non-Voters in 2008 and 2011 General Elections: Findings from New Zealand General Social Survey', Statistics New Zealand, January 2014, http://www.stats.govt.nz/~/media/Statistics/browse-categories/people-and-communities/well-being/civic-hum-rights/non-voters-2008-2011-gen-elections.pdf (accessed 23 August 2015).

17   Ibid.

18   RadioLive, 'Intellectualism.'

19   'Student Loan Scheme Annual Report 2014', Ministry of Education, Wellington, 2014, p.22.

20   Flood, 'Eleanor Catton Blasts Critics.'

Chapter 3

1   'Pat' isn't his real name. I'd like to have asked if he minds my referring to him by name, but we've fallen out of touch.

2   'Household Labour Force Survey: Persons Employed by Employment Status by Industry', Statistics New Zealand, March 2010, http://www.stats.govt.nz/browse_for_stats/income-and-work/employment_and_unemployment/Household LabourForceSurvey_HOTPMar10qtr.aspx (accessed 9 February 2016). (Includes wage or salary earners, employers and the self-employed.)

3   'Long-term data series: Employment by sector', Statistics New Zealand, http://www.stats.govt.nz/browse_for_stats/economic_indicators/NationalAccounts/long-term-data-series/labour-market.aspx (accessed 9 February 2016).

4   Household Labour Force Survey, December 2015.

5   'Earnings and Employment Survey: Filled Jobs by Industry by Sex and Status in Employment', Statistics New Zealand.

6   'National Accounts - SNA 2008: GDP(I)', Statistics New Zealand. Series deflated with the Consumer Price Index and New Zealand's usually resident population.

7   'Earnings and Employment Survey: Average Hourly Earnings by Industry and Sex', Statistics New Zealand. Series deflated with the Consumer Price Index.

8   'New Zealand Census of

Population and Dwellings',
Statistics New Zealand.

9 International Labour
Organisation, *Employees by sex
and economic activity*.

10 Capital–income ratios from
Thomas Piketty's *Capital in
the Twenty-First Century*,
Bellknap Press, Cambridge
Massachusetts, 2014; GDP
figures from the OECD's
national accounts.

11 'Earnings and Employment
Survey: Filled Jobs by
Industry by Sex and Status in
Employment', Statistics New
Zealand.

12 Determining exactly which
payments a universal income
should replace is interesting,
controversial and – at this
point – entirely premature.
The \$20 billion figure includes
superannuation, student
allowances, Working for
Families, the unemployment
benefit, sole parent support,
accommodation assistance,
social housing and Kiwisaver.
Data from Budget 2015.

13 'National Accounts (Income
and Expenditure): Year
ended March 2015', Statistics
New Zealand. Statistics New
Zealand term capital income
'operating surplus' and
depreciation 'consumption

of fixed capital'. The figure
given is after subtracting
depreciation.

14 Fund Rankings, Sovereign
Wealth Fund Institute.
Converted to New Zealand
dollars.

15 Karl Marx, *The Poverty of
Philosophy*.

Chapter 4

1 Arundhati Roy, *Broken
Republic: Three Essays*,
Penguin Books, London, 2011,
ch. 3.

2 Ben Adler, 'Here's What You
Need to Know About the New
Paris Climate Agreement',
Grist, 12 December 2015,
http://grist.org/climate-
energy/heres-what-you-need-
to-know-about-the-new-paris-
climate-agreement (accessed
11 February 2016).

3 Bryan Gould quoted in the
documentary *Hot Air*, directed
by Alister Barry and Abi King-
Jones, 2014.

4 Jane Kelsey, *The FIRE
Economy*, Bridget Williams
Books, Wellington, 2015, ch. 5.

5 'Big Business Turns to Long-
time UK Climate Sceptic',
Greenpeace, 15 November
2007, http://www.greenpeace.
org/new-zealand/en/press/
big-business-turns-to-long-

tim/ (accessed 15 January 2016).

6 'New Zealand's Greenhouse Gas Inventory', Ministry for the Environment, April 2015, https://www.mfe.govt.nz/sites/default/files/media/Climate%20Change/nz-greenhouse-gas-inventory-snapshot-2015.pdf (accessed 15 January 2016).

7 A significant body of research details how these high prices were driven not by market fundamentals but commodity futures speculation, the result of financial deregulation in US and EU financial markets.

8 The Sustainability Council, 'The Carbon Budget Deficit', September 2012, p.19, http://www.sustainabilitynz.org/wp-content/uploads/2013/02/TheCarbonBudgetDeficit.pdf (accessed 4 February 2016).

9 Ibid., pp.20–21.

10 Vernon Small and Olivia Wannan, 'Tim Groser Commits New Zealand to 11pc Cut in Greenhouse Gases', Stuff, 7 July 2015, http://www.stuff.co.nz/national/politics/70038782/climate-change-issues-minister-tim-groser-commits-new-zealand-to-30pc-cut-in-greenhouse-gases (accessed 15 January 2016).

11 Maureen Farrell, '2015 Becomes the Biggest M&A Year Ever', Wall Street Journal, http://www.wsj.com/articles/2015-becomes-the-biggest-m-a-year-ever-1449187101 (accessed 15 January 2016).

12 As the Paris talks played out, US mining giant Anglo American, one of the world's largest coal producers, announced it was cutting two-thirds of its workforce, 85,000 jobs.

13 The author wishes to acknowledge that from 2012 to 2015 he was active in the New Zealand struggle against the TPPA, acting as co-ordinator and spokesperson for the It's Our Future coalition that has actively educated and organised against the agreement, including numerous large-scale street protests.

14 It has just been announced that the investor Transcanada is now launching an investment dispute under the investment chapter of the North American Trade Agreement seeking US$15 billion in damages, provisions similar to those found in the TPPA.

Chapter 5

1   'What It's Like to be Young and Unemployed in New Zealand', The Wireless, 26 May 2015, http://thewireless.co.nz/articles/what-it-s-like-to-be-young-and-unemployed-in-new-zealand (accessed 14 January 2016).

2   New Zealand Council of Trade Unions, 'Under Pressure: a Detailed Report into Insecure Work in New Zealand', Wellington, New Zealand, October 2013, p.2.

3   This name and others in this chapter have been changed to protect the interviewees' identities.

4   Catherine Harris, 'Focus on Stress at Work to Grow', Stuff, 24 March 2014, http://www.stuff.co.nz/business/industries/9859149/Focus-on-stress-at-work-to-grow (accessed 23 February 2016).

5   Danny Dorling, 'Danny Dorling: If You are Young in Britain Today, You are Being Taken for a Ride', *New Statesman*, 7 November 2013, http://www.newstatesman.com/2013/10/defrauding-young-britain (accessed 24 December 2015).

6   Radio New Zealand, 'Thousands losing benefits due to paperwork', http://www.radionz.co.nz/news/national/278454/thousands-losing-benefits-due-to-paperwork (accessed 24 December 2015).

7   Ibid.

8   George Monbiot, 'Curb your Malthusiasm', http://www.monbiot.com/2015/06/23/curb-your-malthusiasm/ (accessed 24 December 2015).

9   'Social Bonds – New Zealand Pilot', Ministry of Health, http://www.health.govt.nz/our-work/preventative-health-wellness/social-bonds-new-zealand-pilot (accessed 24 December 2015).

10   Nicole Mathewson, 'Waitress Unfairly Sacked for Not Smiling Awarded $11,000 in Compensation', Stuff, 13 August 2015, http://www.stuff.co.nz/business/better-business/71079813/Waitress-unfairly-sacked-for-not-smiling-awarded-11-000-in-compensation (accessed 24 December 2015).

11   Patrict McGeehan, 'New York Plans $15-an-Hour Minimum Wage for Fast Food Workers', *New York Times*, 22 July 2015, http://www.nytimes.com/2015/07/23/nyregion/new-york-minimum-wage-

fast-food-workers.html?_r=0
(accessed 24 December 2015).

Chapter 6

1   A. Mikaere, 'From Kaupapa
    Māori Research to Re-
    searching Kaupapa Māori:
    Making Our Contribution
    to Māori Survival', paper
    presented at Kei Tua o Te
    Pae hui, *The Challenges of
    Kaupapa Māori Research in the
    21st Century*, Wellington, 2011,
    p.37.

2   Maori Marsden,
    'Kaitiakitanga: A Definitive
    Introduction to the Holistic
    World View of the Maori',
    November 1992, <www.
    marinenz.org.nz/documents/
    Marsden_1992_Kaitiakitanga.
    pdf>, p.14.

3   L. Pihama, 'Kaupapa Māori
    Theory: Transforming Theory
    in Aotearoa', *He Pukenga
    Korero: A Journal of Māori
    Studies*, Raumati (Summer), 9,
    2 (2010) p.5.

4   L. T. Smith, 'Story-ing the
    Development of Kaupapa
    Māori – a Review of Sorts,'
    paper presented at Kei Tua o
    Te Pae hui, *The Challenges of
    Kaupapa Māori Research in the
    21st Century*, Wellington, 2011,
    p.10.

5   'A guide to the principles of
    the Treaty of Waitangi as
    expressed by the Courts and
    the Waitangi Tribunal', Te
    Puni Kōkiri, 2001, p.19.

6   R. Mihaere, 'A Kaupapa Māori
    Analysis of the Use of Māori
    Cultural Identity in the Prison
    System', PhD thesis, Victoria
    University of Wellington, 2015,
    p.57.

7   Ibid.

8   *New Zealand Maori Council
    v Attorney-General* [1987] 1
    NZLR 641.

9   A. Mikaere, *Colonising Myths
    Māori Realities: He Rukuruku
    Whakaaro*, Huia Publishers,
    Wellington, 2011, pp.123–146.

10 Carwyn Jones, Claire
    Charters, Andrew Erueti
    and Jane Kelsey, 'Expert
    Paper #3: Māori Rights, Te
    Tiriti O Waitangi and the
    Trans-Pacific Partnership
    Agreement', Trans-Pacific
    Partnership Agreement New
    Zealand Expert Paper Series,
    20 January 2016, <https://
    tpplegal.files.wordpress.
    com/2015/12/ep3-tiriti-paper.

11 'Article 29.6: Treaty of
    Waitangi: 1. Provided that
    such measures are not used
    as a means of arbitrary or
    unjustified discrimination
    against persons of the other
    Parties or as a disguised
    restriction on trade in

goods, trade in services and investment, nothing in this Agreement shall preclude the adoption by New Zealand of measures it deems necessary to accord more favourable treatment to Maori in respect of matters covered by this Agreement, including in fulfilment of its obligations under the Treaty of Waitangi.' Trans Pacific Partnership text, New Zealand Foreign Affairs and Trade, https://www.tpp.mfat.govt.nz/text (last accessed 12 February 2016).

12 'Principles of Kaupapa Māori' citing Leonie Pihama, Rangahau, http://rangahau.co.nz/research-idea/27/.

13 Mikaere, *Colonising Myths*, p.126.

14 Te Kawehau Hoskins, 'A Fine Risk: Ethics in Kaupapa Māori Politics', 47(2) *New Zealand Journal of Educational Studies*, 85 (2012), p.87.

15 I do not assert here that Te Tiriti or He Whakaputanga are of no value but reiterate that our rights as Māori are sourced in our histories that precede the signing of Pākehā-introduced instruments.

16 Graham Hingaroa Smith, 'Tane-nui-a-rangi's Legacy: Propping Up the Sky (Kaupapa Maori as Resistance and Intervention)', paper presented at New Zealand Association for Research in Education/Australian Association for Research in Education Joint Conference, Deakin University, Australia, 2012, p.1.

17 Hoskins, p.85.

18 Kaapua Smith, personal communication, 28 August 2015.

19 'Principles of Kaupapa Māori', Rangahau.

20 Mikaere, *Colonising Myths*, pp.29–37.

21 L. Pihama, 'Maori Control Over Maori Frameworks – Why I Advocate Strongly for Kaupapa Maori', Te Wharepora Hou, 26 April 2013, <https://tewhareporahou.wordpress.com/2013/04/26/maori-control-over-maori-frameworks-why-i-advocate-strongly-for-kaupapa-maori/>.

22 Hoskins, *A fine risk*, p.95.

23 K. Smith, personal communication, 2015.

24 Hoskins, *A fine risk*, p.91.

25 'Principles of Kaupapa Māori', Rangahau.

26 Hoskins, *A fine risk*, p.91.

27 Garrick Cooper, 'Kaupapa

Māori Research: Epistemic Wilderness as Freedom?', 47 (2), *New Zealand Journal of Educational Studies*, 64, 2012, pp.64-71.

28 'Principles of Kaupapa Māori', Rangahau.

29 Kevin Carson, 'Mutualism.org: Free Market Anti-Capitalism (introduction)', www.mutualist.org, (accessed 22 August 2015).

30 'Principles of Kaupapa Māori', Rangahau.

31 Carson, 'Mutualism'.

32 Carson, 'Mutualism'.

33 Claudia Orange, 'Treaty of Waitangi', Te Ara – the Encyclopedia of New Zealand, http://www.TeAra.govt.nz/en/treaty-of-waitangi (accessed 22 August 2015).

34 Carson, 'Mutualism'.

35 Mikaere, *Colonising Myths*, pp.35-36.

36 Statism refers to societies in which the state controls social and economic policy.

37 Carson, 'Mutualism'.

38 E. T. Durie, 'Te hono ki Hawai'iki: The Bond with the Pacific', in Margaret Wilson and Paul Hunt (eds), *Culture, Rights and Cultural Rights: Perspectives from the South Pacific*, Huia Publishers, Wellington, 1998, p.50.

39 Hoskins citing Durie, 'Custom Law', unpublished paper, p.93.

40 R. Himona, 'Maori Policy: Whanau, Hapu, Iwi Mythology', Te Putatara, 29 July 2013, www.putatara.net/2013/07/whanau-hapu-iwi/ (accessed 16 January 2015).

41 Mikaere, *Colonising Myths*, p.33.

42 Hoskins, *A fine risk*, p.86.

43 Carson, 'Mutualism'.

44 'Interview: Labour Leader David Cunliffe', Newshub, 21 September 2014, www.3news.co.nz/tvshows/thenation/interview-labour-leader-david-cunliffe-2014091313#axzz3imahpAtz (last accessed 16 January 2015).

45 Ibid.

46 'Native Affairs – Labour's New Leader David Cunliffe', Māori Television, 16 September 2013, www.maoritelevision.com/news/politics/native-affairs-labours-new-leader-david-cunliffe (last accessed 16 January 2015).

47 Elizabeth Strickett, 'Marginalising Maori Adolescent Parents', literature review, Massey University, 2012, p.5.

48 Hoskins, *A fine risk*, p.95.

49 Mikaere, *Colonising Myths*, p.30.

50 Mamari Stephens, 'Confessions of a Moderate Maori Voter … (If that's OK with you, that is)', Tangatawhenua.com, 30 August 2014, http://sparrowhawkkarearea.com/2014/08/30/confessions-of-a-moderate-maori-voter-if-thats-ok-with-you-that-is/ (accessed 16 January 2015).

51 Mikaere, *Colonising Myths*, p.30.

Chapter 7

1 After 2005, the children of non-citizens do not get automatic citizenship even if they are born in New Zealand.

2 Cisgender refers to people whose gender, from the perspective of prevailing social norms, is aligned to their sex.

Chapter 9

1 Pope Francis, *Laudato si': On Care for Our Common Home*, Vatican City, 24 May 2015.

2 Ibid., p.71.

3 Ibid., p.154.

4 Ibid., p.41.

5 Ibid., p.35.

6 Ibid., p.142.

7 Ibid., p.86.

8 Ibid., p.10.

9 Ibid., p.146.

10 Pope Francis, *Evangelii Gaudium*, Vatican City, December 2013, p.76.

11 *Laudato si'*, p.52.

12 Ibid.

13 *Laudato si'*, p.65.

14 Ibid., p.158.

15 Naomi Klein, 'A Radical Vatican?, *New Yorker*, 10 July 2015, http://www.newyorker.com/news/news-desk/a-visit-to-the-vatican (accessed 23 November 2015).

16 *Laudato si'*, p.157.

17 Ibid., p.168.

Chapter 10

1 I am grateful to Philip McKibbin, with whom I first developed the idea of 'the politics of love': Max Harris and Philip McKibbin, 'The Politics of Love', The Aotearoa Project, 20 May 2015, https://theaotearoaproject.wordpress.com/2015/05/20/the-politics-of-love-max-harris-and-philip-mckibbin/ (accessed 6 September 2015).

2 George Monbiot, 'The Age of Loneliness is Killing Us', *Guardian*, 14 October 2014, http://www.theguardian.com/commentisfree/2014/oct/14/age-of-loneliness-killing-us (accessed 7 September 2015).

3   This is close to the definition used in Harris and McKibbin, although it is slightly altered from the definition used in the original article.

4   Cleve Barlow writes in *Tikanga Whakaaro: Key Concepts in Maori Culture*, Oxford University Press, Melbourne, 2001, 'He aha te aroha? Ko te aroha he tikanga whakaaro nui …' (What is aroha? Aroha is an all-encompassing quality of goodness …) I am indebted to Philip McKibbin for this reference.

5   See 'The Politics of Love', note 1.

6   bell hooks, *All About Love: New Visions*, Harper Perennial, USA, 2013.

7   Martha Nussbaum, *Political Emotions: Why Love Matters for Justice,* Harvard University Press, Cambridge, 2013.

8   Andrew Dean, *Ruth, Roger, and Me,* Bridget Williams Books, Wellington, 2015.

9   Thanks to, amongst others, Mark Bennett for raising this point.

10   Mark Bennett, Hemanth Nair and others have informally articulated versions of this concern.

11   Thanks to James Graham and Julian Ensbey for raising this issue.

12   Jane Kelsey, 'New Zealand "Experiment" a Colossal Failure', 9 July 1999, www.converge.org.nz/pma/apfail.htm (accessed 7 September 2015).

13   Rt. Hon. John Key, 'Next Steps in Social Housing', Beehive.govt.nz, 28 January 2015, https://www.beehive.govt.nz/speech/next-steps-social-housing (accessed 7 September 2015).

14   Rt. Hon. John Key, 'Pre-Budget Speech to Business New Zealand Function', Beehive.govt.nz, 14 April 2015, https://www.beehive.govt.nz/speech/pre-budget-speech-business-new-zealand-function (accessed 7 September 2015).

15   Rt. Hon. John Key, 'Speech to Canterbury Employers' Chamber of Commerce Function', Beehive.govt.nz, 2 July 2015, https://www.beehive.govt.nz/speech/speech-canterbury-employers%E2%80%99-chamber-commerce-function (accessed 7 September 2015).

16   Rt. Hon. John Key, 'Waitangi Day Breakfast Speech', Beehive.govt.nz, 6 February

2015, https://www.beehive. govt.nz/speech/waitangi-day-breakfast-speech; Rt. Hon. John Key, 'Speech at Chunuk Bair', Beehive.govt. nz, 26 April 2015, https:// www.beehive.govt.nz/speech/ speech-chunuk-bair (both last accessed 7 September 2015).

17 Rt. Hon. John Key, 'Speech to Open of [sic] NZ-Dubai Business Seminar at the Dubai Chamber of Commerce', Beehive.govt.nz, 26 April 2015, https://www.beehive. govt.nz/speech/speech-open-nz-dubai-business-seminar-dubai-chamber-commerce (accessed 7 September 2015).

18 Ibid.

19 Rt. Hon. John Key, 'Pre-Budget Speech'.

20 Monbiot, 'The Age of Loneliness'.

21 Monbiot refers to Brian Beach and Sally-Marie Bamford, 'Isolation: The Emerging

Crisis for Older Men', Independent Age, 2014, http:// www.independentage.org/ campaigning/loneliness-and-staying-connected/isolation-a-growing-issue-among-older-men/ (last accessed 7 September 2015).

22 Emily White, 'Loneliness is Not a Private Matter', Guardian, 6 November 2015, http://www.theguardian. com/commentisfree/2015/ nov/06/loneliness-market-society-isolation-income?CMP=share_btn_link (accessed 11 December 2015).

23 Statistics New Zealand: Tatauranga Aotearoa, Loneliness in New Zealand: Findings from the New Zealand General Social Survey, Statistics New Zealand, 2013, p. 5.

24 Ibid, p.11.

25 Ibid, p.12.

26 Ibid.

ABOUT THE AUTHORS

EDITOR

Morgan Godfery is a writer and trade unionist based in Wellington. He is an online columnist for *Overland Literary Journal* in Australia and a regular book reviewer for *Fairfax*. His writing regularly appears in the *Guardian* and the *Herald*. He also appears on radio and television as a political commentator and has authored several academic chapters and lectured extensively on Maori politics. He graduated in law from Victoria University in 2015.

CONTRIBUTORS

Andrew Dean is an Ashburton local based in the United Kingdom. In 2012 he was awarded a Rhodes Scholarship and is currently studying towards a doctorate in English literature at the University of Oxford. He is also the author of *Ruth, Roger and Me,* the acclaimed BWB Text.

Max Harris is an Examination Fellow at All Souls College, Oxford. He has worked as a clerk to Chief Justice Elias in the Supreme Court and his writing has been published in *The New Statesman, openDemocracy, The Huffington Post*, and *The Pantograph Punch*. He's currently working on a book about the future of progressive politics and policy in New Zealand.

Lamia Imam is a Christchurch-born communications consultant based in Austin, Texas. She recently graduated with a Masters in Public Administration from the LBJ School of Public Affairs at the University of Texas at Austin. She has presented at the Congressional Research Service in Washington D.C. on Congressional committees' use of social media and previously worked in Wellington for the Labour Leader's Office and at the Office of Treaty Settlements. She blogs on New Zealand politics at CornerPolitics.com and tweets under the handle @LI_Politico.

Chloe King is a writer and activist based currently based in Auckland. Chloe has been involved in movements for social change and Indigenous rights since she was 14. She holds a post graduate diploma in Visual Arts and Art and Design and is the former editor of *Debate*, the Auckland University of Technology student magazine.

Daniel Kleinsman is a lawyer and activist currently based in the Philippines. He is a dual citizen of New Zealand and the Netherlands. After graduating in law at Victoria University of Wellington in 2014 he worked as an adviser at the Ministry of Business,

Innovation and Employment and is currently training as a Catholic priest.

Edward Miller is a Kuala Lumpur-based campaign advisor for the Building and Wood Workers' International, a global trade union federation. Edward has been widely published, including *Interest. co.nz* and the *Pantograph Punch*, and until late-2015 organised national opposition against the TPPA. He holds undergraduate degrees in law and philosophy and a postgraduate degree in law from the University of Auckland.

Courtney Sina Meredith is a poet, playwright, fiction writer and musician of Samoan, Mangaian and Irish descent. She holds a degree in English and Political Studies from the University of Auckland, where she also co-edited *Spectrum 5*. She is a former writer-in-residence at the Bleibtreu Berlin and her first book of poetry, *Brown Girls in Bright Red Lipstick*, was published in 2012.

Carrie Stoddart-Smith is an Auckland-Wellington commuting senior policy analyst of Ngāti Tautahi, Ngāti Rēhia and Ngāpuhi descent. She holds a BA and LLB from Auckland University and an LLM in International Law and Politics with First Class Honours from the University of Canterbury. She has written extensively on Maori politics.

Wilbur Townsend is a writer and economist based in Wellington. He is a former feature writer for *Salient*, the Victoria University student magazine, and is the winner of the Sir Frank Holmes Prize. In 2015 he graduated with a BA in Economics and Philosophy and a BSc in Mathematics, in 2016 he will complete an MCom in Economics.

Holly Walker is a writer, children's advocate, and former Green MP. In 2005, while at the University of Otago, Holly edited the student magazine *Critic Te Arohi*. After graduating with a BA(hons) in Politics and English she won a Rhodes Scholarship and graduated from the University of Oxford with a Masters in Development Studies. Holly publishes essays and reviews of women writers and co-hosts a parenting podcast.

About BWB Texts

BWB Texts are short books on big subjects: succinct narratives spanning history, memoir, contemporary issues, science and more from great New Zealand writers. All BWB Texts are available digitally, with selected works also in paperback. New Texts are published monthly – please visit www.bwb.co.nz to see the latest releases.

BWB Texts include:

Paul Callaghan: Luminous Moments
Foreword by Catherine Callaghan

Creeks and Kitchens: A Childhood Memoir
Maurice Gee

Report from Christchurch
Rebecca Macfie

Hidden Agendas: What We Need to Know about the TPPA
Jane Kelsey

Geering and God, 1965–71: The Heresy Trial that Divided New Zealand
Lloyd Geering

Inequality and the West
Robert Wade

The Zealandia Drowning Debate: Did New Zealand Sink Beneath the Waves?
Hamish Campbell

The Quiet War on Asylum
Tracey Barnett

What Happened at Waitangi?
Claudia Orange

When the Tour Came to Auckland
Geoff Chapple

Thorndon: Wellington and Home, My Katherine Mansfield Project
Kirsty Gunn

First Contact: Tasman's Arrival in Taitapu, 1642
Anne Salmond

Wellbeing Economics: Future Directions for New Zealand
Paul Dalziel & Caroline Saunders

Growing Apart: Regional Prosperity in New Zealand
Shamubeel Eaqub